Carol Richardson Marty is a Seattle-based, Southern-raised cook, who is an award-winning culinary photographer and cake decorator. Carol has parlayed her love of food and photography into two businesses: Sugar Sand Photography and Carol's Creative Confections. She is an experienced photographer, food stylist, and culinary instructor who has worked with a variety of companies, including Tully's Coffee, Quaker Oatmeal, and Sur La Table. Additionally, Carol is a recipe tester for *Cook's Country* magazine, and a field editor for *Taste of Home* magazine. She is originally from Tallahassee, Florida, is a Florida State University alumna, and is a die-hard FSU football fan!

Karen Binkhorst is a busy and well-respected personal chef and caterer in Seattle, Washington. She has owned her business, Home Meals with Karen, since 1997. Karen received a degree in Restaurant Management from Columbus Technical College in Columbus, Ohio, in 1981, but most of her education has come from working in all kinds of food establishments—from hotels, country clubs, and top restaurants to truck stops. Karen has been inspiring folks to cook by teaching cooking classes to anyone who will listen since 1995. She lives with her two partners Jeri and Jen and intends to never leave paradise.

Every Bite

How to Make
The Most of Your Meals

Carol Richardson Marty and
Karen Binkhorst

Every Bite

How to Make
The Most of Your Meals

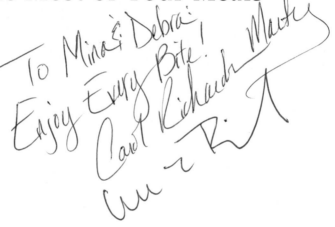

To Mina & Debra:
Enjoy Every Bite!
Carol Richardson Marty

Vanguard Press

VANGUARD PAPERBACK

A CIP catalogue record for this title is
available from the British Library.

ISBN 978 1 84386 746 3

Vanguard Press is an imprint of
Pegasus Elliot MacKenzie Publishers Ltd.

www.pegasuspublishers.com

First Published in 2014

Vanguard Press
Sheraton House Castle Park
Cambridge England

Printed & Bound in Great Britain

Every Bite:
Table of Contents

Karen and Carol would like to dedicate this cookbook to all those who love food and cooking; whether that is those who have cooked many times before, or those who are just finding their way. The best times of our lives are spent around food. We love sharing recipes and ideas that inspire these moments, and hope you enjoy making these recipes as much as we did.

Acknowledgements

Karen and Carol would like to extend a heartfelt thanks to those who contributed with their time, their palate, and their pocketbook. Your support and generosity is so appreciated and we cannot begin to thank you enough.

Karen and Carol would also like to thank Judith Dern for her insight and support in this process, Diane Sepanski and Lisa Gordanier for their editing expertise, and Carol's sister, Jo Anne, who came up with the book title!

Carol would like to thank her husband, Andy, for his support throughout this very exciting but long process! She would also love to thank her family: her father, Walter, her Mom, Jo, and her sisters, Jo Anne and Susan, whose support and love is tremendous. Best family EVER!

Karen would like to thank her partners, Jeri Hudson and Jen Mandel, her friends and family and all the people that helped inspire this cookbook. Love to all.

Thank you to everyone who supported Karen and Carol throughout this exciting journey!

Disclaimer

"No food was wasted in the making of this cookbook"

Menu Planning

The *foundation* of Every Bite

Menu planning is the *foundation* to eating Every Bite. No more liquid vegetables, unidentifiable bags of goo, or scary science projects in your refrigerator. No more wasted time running to the store to pick up that one forgotten ingredient, or throwing out leftovers from the week before because it spoiled. Now is the time to create the habit of menu planning. It saves time, money, food, and effort. We want to share our years of cooking and catering experience with you to help you plan your menus with ease, reduce or eliminate waste, and have awesome variety in your weekly meals!

Getting Started:

Planning your menus starts with a couple of simple steps that are straight forward and intuitive: decide what you want to eat, check to see what you already have on hand (fresh, in the freezer, and in the pantry), and then shop for the remaining ingredients.

When trying to decide on what to eat, simply start with a "general food base", such as chicken, fish or tofu. Maybe something you've used in a previous recipe? When deciding, we always like to ask ourselves: what did we really think about the food and recipe? Did it put a smile on our face?! Did we enjoy making and eating it? Or was it just too much trouble to get everything together and make it? We want food and cooking to be a positive experience for you. So the more we can help you plan and organize, the more we think it will help make that positive experience a reality. If you're somewhat new to the kitchen and don't really have a recipe in mind, never fear! The pages ahead have many options for you to explore!

Many people, particularly those who are just cooking for themselves or for one other person, tend to eat the same things over and over again. Their menus can become uninspired and lacking in variety. Too often, people get into this "food rut" because they feel they don't have enough time to plan, or have the knowledge, skills, or creativity to make interesting meals. We hope that through *Every Bite*, you find your "chef side" and enjoy every minute of it!

When To Plan: A Week's Worth of Good Eating

We recommend outlining your menu plan on a weekly basis to help get into a routine. As a general rule, we like to menu plan on Saturday or Sunday in preparation for the upcoming week. For all your meals (or as many as you want to plan), be sure to first check to see what you already have on hand, and then shop for the remaining ingredients. We know that many times, simply making the decision on what you want to eat or cook can seem daunting, but it doesn't have to be. Simply put, planning saves.

Checking what you have in the refrigerator, freezer and/or pantry first is the easiest way *not* to waste food. It only takes a few extra minutes to look in the back of that pantry and freezer, and more often than you think, you'll find something you forgot was in there! We encourage you to buy fresh organic vegetables and pasture-raised meats when possible for its additional health benefits (in many cases, frozen organic vegetables will work and often the cost is more stable). We are big proponents of buying the BEST food that you can get. You will be more satisfied with ingredients (especially pantry ingredients) that are full of flavor and nutrition than some cheap, barely palatable "food" found in the back reaches of a "specials" bin. It's more expensive to buy the better food, but in the end it saves on waste and gives way more satisfaction and enjoyment to your meals.

Menu planning and an overall awareness of the food and what you're buying helps eliminate redundancy, and leads to less waste. For example, how many times have you bought cilantro for a recipe and needed only a quarter of the bunch? What did you do with the rest? Chances are you wasted it; not from lack of caring, but from lack of knowledge. We address these issues in each recipe. For example, you might use some later in the week for your Asian-Style Pork Baguettes with Carrot Slaw (see page 75), or simply mince and mix it with a touch of oil and freeze it for use at a later date.

Prepping Ahead

Putting the _action_ into Every Bite

So you've planned your menu, and gone shopping… now what? Now you prep as much as possible for the meals you've planned. Not wasting time is just as important as not wasting effort or food.

Step one—mince, chop, peel, and dice anything you can ahead of time because it is a huge timesaver during the week. You can do this for almost anything (except lettuces and herbs) and up to 4 days ahead of time. Try and use glass containers for storage because it doesn't off-gas like plastic can.

If you're making recipes with meat in them, you will get more flavor if you salt and pepper it a day or two ahead. Doing this allows the cells in the meat to draw the salt in so that the meat is seasoned essentially from the inside out. Don't worry: it won't taste salty! It's a similar technique to brining without the sugar or soaking.

Step two—Group your ingredients together according to the recipe. Keep the vegetables in bags in the crisper drawer and dry ingredients in the cupboard.

Step three—cook and enjoy!

Prepping Herbs and Spices: Helpful Tips and Ideas

What is an herb? An herb is the fragrant leaf of annual or perennial plants.

What is a spice? A spice is the dried stem, bark, seed or root of a plant.

Whichever you use in a recipe, make sure that the herb or spice is fragrant to get its full flavor potential. You can use either fresh or dried herbs, but keep in mind that dried herbs are more potent and concentrated, so you'll need to use **less** in a recipe. The ratio of dried to fresh herbs is 1:3. For example, if a recipe calls for 1 tablespoon of fresh dill and you only have dried dill on hand, just use 1 teaspoon (because 3 teaspoons=1 tablespoon).

When buying dry herbs and spices, buy in small amounts and whole if possible. If you are buying a blend (like curry or Italian seasonings) buy a few tablespoons at a time and store in tight fitting bottles that have been dated. Store in a dark area like a drawer or a cabinet. Dry herbs and spices that have been ground lose their potency after about six months. If the spice is whole (like nutmeg, cloves or peppercorns), then it keeps almost indefinitely. This really pays off when buying seasonal spices like cloves or nutmeg. Sometimes it's attractive to buy ground herbs and spices in big jars or in bulk, but it will most likely lose their flavor before you can use it all, and then food and money has been wasted. Just remember: in general, bulk foods are a great, inexpensive way to go; only buy what you need.

If the recipe calls for fresh herbs, don't chop or mince them until it's time to make the recipe. This will keep them fresher longer. If you have more fresh herbs than you'll need, mince the extras, add a teaspoon of olive oil per quarter cup of minced herbs and freeze them in small ice cube trays or in small, "snack" sized re-sealable bags. Write the date and name of the herb on the bag so you're not trying to figure out what's what later! Keep in mind that fresh herbs only stay "fresh" in the freezer for about one month. Keep a list nearby of what's in the freezer so you'll know what you have next time you're prepping ahead for the week.

If you're using dry herbs, keep in mind that you can almost always substitute dry herbs instead of fresh _except_ when you make a fresh only salad (like a caprese salad) or maybe in a dish where fresh herbs are added at the last moment before serving. That would not be tasty in either flavor or in the mouth. It's best to heat dry herbs to activate the volatile oil's (that's the flavor in the herb) release into the dish. It is best to add them early in the cooking process. If cooking with fresh herbs however, the flavor dissipates quickly, so add it in just before serving so you get the fresh herby flavor right before you eat! (an exception is Italian parsley: it can be added in the beginning of the cooking process)

Another great tip for using up any extra dried herbs is to make an infused oil. To make basil oil for example, heat your leftover, whole basil leaves, and stems with one cup of safflower or canola oil on low heat for fifteen minutes (olive will work for some, but tends to go rancid quicker, and safflower and canola are more of a "tasteless" oil, that provides a nice base for an infusion). Turn off and let the basil flavor infuse into the oil for six to eight hours. Strain the basil from the oil, using a sieve or cheesecloth.

Store in a tightly closed bottle that is labeled and dated in the refrigerator. In the refrigerator, the infused oil will remain fresh for about 2 months. You can use that technique with lots of different dry herbs. Infused oils are great in salad dressing and other places where you want a "blast" of flavor.

Storing Fresh Herbs

Some herbs like basil don't like to be very cold. It's best to snip one half inch off the bottom of the stems put them in a glass with one inch of water (much like you keep flowers fresh in a vase). Store on the counter in a cooler but not cold area.
Other herbs like cilantro or Italian parsley can be washed and spun in a salad spinner or gently patted dry in a towel. Wrap the stem ends in a moist paper towel, place in a re-sealable bag, and keep in the crisper drawer. Fresh herbs stored like this will keep about seven days; plenty of time to use them up!

Freezing Herbs

You can also freeze cilantro and parsley stems whole to use in a later recipe. If you just throw them in the freezer, when you go to take them out, they will be all mushy and brown. Eww! To prevent that, you simply need to blanch them (see our instructional blanching video at
http://karenandcaroleverybite.wordpress.com), dry them off, put in a re-sealable bag, label and date, and then throw them in the freezer. When they come out of the freezer for your next recipe: nothing but green goodness!

Notes About the Cookbook and General Layout

This cookbook is different from others in that we take a totally different approach to the chapters. Instead of having chapters such as "appetizers", "soups", and "desserts", we have chapters that start with a main ingredient (such as chicken) and subsequent recipes within that chapter are based on and use ingredients from that first recipe.

At the end of most of the chapters, is a *"Last Bite"* recipe. This is a "clean up" recipe to use all the ends and pieces of the ingredients from previous recipes as possible.

Also at the end of each chapter is a blank page for you to write down any notes and/or comments you have from the chapter's recipes.

Many recipes have a "Note(s) From Within Recipe" section. This section is to help you along with tips, ideas, and clarification based on certain parts of the recipe. We also include gluten-free options throughout when we know of one that works, but feel free to add your own gluten-free option where you can!

And lastly are our *"Flavor Blast"* additions. Within many of the recipes, we have what we call *"Flavor Blast"* ingredients. These give the recipe that extra kick, and really bump up the flavor! We hope you'll enjoy the *Blasts*!

Now you're ready to begin cooking and eating Every Bite!

Chapter 1

Calling All Fowl: Bawk, Bawk Chicken!

Perfect Roasted Chicken

Yield: One 3-pound chicken

The name says it all: perfectly moist and flavorful, this roasted chicken never fails to please! Balsamic Glazed Carrots (see recipe page 159) would pair nicely with this.

Note that you can always use a couple of game hens in this recipe as an alternative to the chicken.

1 (3-pound) chicken, organic and pasture-raised, if possible
10 sprigs fresh Italian parsley, leaves minced and stems reserved (about 2 slightly heaping tablespoons of leaves)
8 fresh basil leaves, minced and stems reserved (about 2½ slightly heaping tablespoons of leaves)
6 tablespoons butter, softened
1 lemon
1¼ teaspoons salt, divided
½ teaspoon plus 1/8 teaspoon freshly ground pepper, divided
2 cloves minced garlic
4 cloves garlic, smashed flat as a piece of paper

Preheat the oven to 475°F. Line a cookie sheet or jelly roll pan with aluminum foil.

Remove the chicken from its wrapper, and remove everything from within the cavity: large pieces of fat, neck, gizzard, and liver. It's best not to save or use the liver unless it's from an organic chicken—it's a filter organ and can be contaminated, so it's safer not to eat it.* Save the other cavity contents, except the fat, for making The Best Homemade Chicken Stock (page 36).

In a separate pan the fat can be cooked down at low heat until all the fat is rendered, reserve to a storage jar and keep in the fridge for later use in sautéing or adding that extra "something". This is called Schmaltz and has been used forever.

Pat the chicken dry, inside and out, with paper towels. Do not rinse it, as this can contaminate your sink area with splatter from the water.**

Place the parsley and basil stems on the pan, then set the chicken on top of the stems.*** Put the butter in a small mixing bowl. Grate 1 tablespoon of lemon zest (which should be the amount you get from the one lemon) and add it to the butter. Be sure to only use the colored part of the peel, as the white part just underneath the peel is bitter.

Add the minced herbs, 1 teaspoon of the salt, ½ teaspoon of the pepper, and the minced garlic. Using a fork, mash and thoroughly stir the butter together until everything is evenly distributed.

Place the smashed garlic inside the chicken cavity. Cut the zested lemon into quarters, squeeze the juice from each quarter into the cavity, and then toss the lemon pieces into the cavity.

Gently loosen the skin of the legs and breasts by taking your index finger and gently lifting the skin up and away from the meat itself, being careful not to tear the skin. Stuff half of the butter mixture underneath the skin on one side (all around on the breast and down onto the leg and thigh). Place the other half of the butter mixture underneath the other breast, leg and thigh. Tuck the wings underneath the shoulders of the chicken by bending the tip ends under the wing so they lie flat. Sprinkle the remaining ¼ teaspoon salt and 1/8 teaspoon pepper on top.

Roast the chicken for 40 minutes, or until the internal temperature reads 160°F on an instant-read meat thermometer. While a meat thermometer is a must-have tool and is best for the most accurate determination of when your chicken is properly cooked, you can also press the chicken at the breast area and it should have some give.****

Remove the chicken from the oven and transfer it to a plate. Let it sit for 5 minutes before slicing. Save the leftover meat for the other delicious recipes in this chapter (or other recipes you enjoy). It can be refrigerated for 4–5 days or frozen for a month. The carcass and cavity parts can also be frozen for 1–3 months; until you're ready to make stock.

Notes From Within Recipe

*The liver is small, dark, and soft. If you're unsure what part is the liver, don't save anything. You'll still be able to have a wonderful chicken stock with the carcass of the chicken after you're finished with this recipe.

**Washing/rinsing the bird can potentially spread any bacteria that might be on the chicken. The chicken will cook at a high enough temperature and for a long enough time to kill off any potentially harmful bacteria. Patting the chicken dry and removing as much moisture as possible will help it roast and brown nicely in the oven.

***Using the stems in this way serves several functions: 1) it utilizes leftovers so there is minimal waste involved, 2) setting the bird on the stems lifts them up a bit and helps everything cook more evenly, and 3) it provides more flavor to infuse into the meat.

****Be sure to take the temperature at the thickest part of the thigh, trying not to hit any bone. You can check the temperature at a few different places to confirm it.

See the video on our blog at *http://karenandcaroleverybite.wordpress.com* on how to assess the temperature of your roasted chicken.

Herbed Chicken & Broccoli Quiche

Yield: One 9-inch quiche, or about 12 muffin-size mini quiches

A great make-ahead meal, this is perfect as a grab & go lunch, a hearty breakfast, or a wonderful light dinner, paired with a salad. You can also bake this recipe in muffin tins to make mini quiches, which are easy to eat and store. Everyone, including real men, will love this winner!

½ recipe Fabulous Flaky Pie Crust (see recipe page 198)*

1 cup chopped Perfect Roasted Chicken (see recipe page 27)

1 cup chopped, cooked fresh broccoli (or frozen); completely thawed and patted dry**

4 large eggs

1¾ cups half-and-half

1 teaspoon salt

½ teaspoon pepper

5 ounces softened garlic-and-herb whipped cream cheese spread, divided

Fresh chopped herbs such as thyme, chives, basil, or parsley (optional)

Preheat the oven to 400°F.

Roll the pastry out into a circle just larger than your pie plate. (For example, if you're using a 9-inch pie plate, roll the crust out into a circle 10 inches in diameter.) Place the crust in the plate, place a piece of parchment paper on top of the pastry, and add pie weights*** on top of the parchment.

Put the pie plate on a large baking sheet or jelly roll pan, and bake the crust for 20 minutes.**** Remove the pan from the oven, and remove the pie weights and parchment from the crust. Leave the oven on 400°F to bake the quiche. Sprinkle the chicken and broccoli around in the crust.
In a medium bowl, whisk the eggs, half-and-half, salt, pepper, ½ of the herbed cream cheese spread*****, and herbs (if using) until well blended. Pour the mixture into the crust.

Once the filling is in the crust, drop the other ½ of the herbed cream cheese by teaspoonfuls all around the top of the quiche (do not do this if making the mini-quiches; see note at end of recipe for clarification). Cover the crust edge with strips of aluminum foil or a pie shield to prevent excessive browning during baking. Bake the quiche for 10 minutes at 400°F, and then reduce the oven temperature to 325°F. Bake the quiche for an additional 35 minutes, or until a knife inserted in the center comes out clean. Remove the foil, and let the quiche stand for 15 minutes before serving.

Notes From Within Recipe

*You can freeze the other half of the pie crust recipe (or one crust worth) in the freezer for up to 2 months.

**See our video blog post (*http://karenandcaroleverybite.wordpress.com*) on blanching broccoli and other kinds of vegetables!

****Pie weights are sold at kitchen and housewares stores. They can be either individual weights that look like small, round, clay stones, or tied together on a metal string. If you don't have pie weights, you can also use dried beans or even pennies! The idea is the same with whatever you use: you need something that can withstand the oven heat with some weight to it so it holds the crust down so it doesn't puff up.

****This method is called blind baking, which means to prebake a crust before adding the filling. It is necessary when the crust will be filled with an unbaked filling (such as with pudding or cream pies), or when the filling has a shorter baking time than the crust. Blind-baking the crust also helps prevent it from becoming soggy from its filling.

*****If making the 9-inch quiche, make sure to split the cream cheese spread. Half goes into the egg mixture, and the other half is dropped on top, as mentioned in the recipe. However, if you are making the mini quiches, add all of the herbed cream cheese into the egg mixture. Due to the size of the smaller quiches, it works better to have the cream cheese all mixed in together with the egg mixture.

Walnut-Chicken Salad with Strawberries

Yield: 2 lunch servings

A delicious, flavorful, and crunchy salad with the zip of lemon and ginger. These flavors will brighten not only a warm summer day, but even a dark winter afternoon. If possible, make the dressing an hour or so ahead so the flavors have time to blend well together.

For the dressing:

2 tablespoons mayonnaise (low-fat is fine)

2 tablespoons Greek-style plain yogurt*

1 tablespoon freshly squeezed lemon juice

½ teaspoon sugar

½ teaspoon ground ginger

Dash salt

For the salad:

¾ cup chopped Perfect Roasted Chicken (see recipe page 27)

¾ cup finely chopped celery—about 1 rib

2 tablespoons walnuts, toasted and chopped

¼ cup chopped strawberries

2 cups bite-size pieces romaine lettuce

Combine all the dressing ingredients in a small bowl and mix well. Set the dressing aside so the flavors have time to meld together while you finish making the rest of the salad.

In a medium bowl, stir together the chicken, celery, and toasted walnuts and toss with the dressing. Gently fold in the strawberries. Place the lettuce on a plate, top with the chicken/strawberry mixture, and enjoy!

Note From Within Recipe

*If you buy a small container of the yogurt, be sure to save what's leftover and use it in the Tasty Tacos recipe in chapter 4!

Chicken-Stuffed Pastry Pockets

Yield: 6 medium pastry pockets

These pockets are a little cheesy, a little crunchy, and a lot flavorful—all packed in a light, flaky crust.

½ recipe Fabulous Flaky Pie Crust (see recipe page 198)*

Per pocket:

¼ cup finely chopped Perfect Roasted Chicken (see recipe page 27), about ¼-inch pieces
1 tablespoon softened garlic-and-herb whipped cream cheese spread
1½ tablespoons Zippy Tomato Sauce (see recipe page 196), or other good canned variety
Milk or water, for brushing the pastry

Preheat the oven to 375°F.

On a lightly floured surface, roll the pastry out to about 1/8-inch thickness. Using a biscuit cutter, cut out circles approximately 6 inches in diameter.

For each pastry pocket, mix together the chicken, cheese, and tomato sauce. Place the mixture on one side of the circle, being sure to leave about a 1-inch border around the edge (to allow room for folding it over).

Lightly brush the pastry with water around the 1-inch border you've just left open. Fold the pastry over the filling into a half-moon shape, and press down all around the edges to make sure they're thoroughly sealed. Crimp the edges with a fork. This will complete the seal and make attractive indentations.

Place the pockets on a parchment paper or Silpat-lined baking sheet. Brush the top of each pocket lightly with milk to help it brown. Cut three ½-inch slits in the top of each pocket to allow steam to escape.

Bake the pockets for 25 minutes, or until they're golden brown. Let them cool for 5 minutes before serving—the insides of the pockets will be piping hot!

Note From Within Recipe

You can freeze the other half of the pie crust recipe (or one crust worth) in the freezer for up to 2 months.

The Best Homemade Chicken Stock

Yield: 2 to 3 quarts

Being able to make a good stock is one of the most important cooking techniques you can learn. Stock is one of the true foundations of cooking, and its uses are limitless—it's the blank canvas on which to create your masterpiece.

Start with a large stockpot (at least 4 quarts) with a colander basket. Add any and all chicken parts except the liver and fat. This can include both the raw pieces you removed from the cavity of the whole chicken, as well as the cooked chicken carcass from the Perfect Roast Chicken recipe on page 27 (cooked or roasted chicken will make a richer stock).

Add a variety of flavorful ingredients, including any or all of the following:
Onion skins (and ends): about a cup
Carrot peels and ends: about a cup
Garlic skins and ends: about ¼ cup
Bay leaf (1), parsley stems, thyme stems and leaves, peppercorns, rosemary stems and leaves: about a handful
Stick with the perennial herbs instead of the softer annuals; they'll infuse a better, long-lasting flavor.
Celery ends: about a cup
Tomato cores and scraps: about ½ cup
Mushroom ends, peels, and stems: about ½ cup

Do not add squash, bell peppers, red onions, livers, or citrus: they will either cloud the stock or make it bitter

Cover everything with cold water* and bring it to a boil, then immediately reduce the heat to a simmer—you want it barely high enough to have "lazy" bubbles ("lazy" bubbles are small bubbles around the edge of the pot. Basically you want a soft, gentle bubbling, not a full rolling boil). You can see our video blog (*http://karenandcaroleverybite.wordpress.com*) on various stages of boiling water.

Cook the stock for 45 minutes (minimum) to 3 hours (maximum). While it simmers, periodically skim off the scum and any fat that has come to the top. **<u>Do not stir the stock!</u>****

You'll know the stock is done when it smells great, has a clear, golden color and will have a rich, robust smell. If you are using a colander basket just lift the colander. If you are not using a colander, use a ladle to remove the larger pieces of chicken and vegetables. Carefully strain the stock through a fine sieve or a cheesecloth-lined colander to clean out any last impurities. What you are left with is a glorious, richly flavored broth.

The stock can be frozen for one to two months. Freeze in different-sized containers for different dishes, such as ice cube trays for sauces, deglazing, or sautéed dishes, and a quart tub for soups, polenta, or risotto.

You can also save the fat that you have skimmed off throughout the cooking process by chilling the bowl into which you've placed the fat and scum. The fat will harden and can be stored in the refrigerator for up to 2 weeks, for use in another recipe later.***

Notes From Within Recipe

*Through the cooking process, cold water draws out the chicken bones' natural albumin (water-soluble protein). This lifts any impurities up to the top, creating a scum of coagulated protein, which can then be skimmed off with a ladle and discarded.
**The whole idea behind skimming is to remove impurities. By stirring, you agitate everything—impurities included, and that's not what we want.

***Rendered chicken fat is also called *schmaltz* (Yiddish term) and can be made from the actual fat, the fat under the skin, or from the stock skimmings. All are delicious.

Last Bite Recipe: Chicken Tortilla Soup

Yield: 2 servings

This soup is a great way to use up all your roasted chicken, as well as clean out some of the veggies still in the fridge. It's pretty darn tasty too!

1 tablespoon vegetable oil

¼ cup finely diced onion

2 tablespoons finely diced celery

2 cloves minced garlic

½ cup to ¾ cup shredded Perfect Roasted Chicken (see recipe page 27)

Flavor Blast!

½ teaspoon ground cumin

½ teaspoon sweet paprika

¼ teaspoon dried oregano

1/8 teaspoon freshly ground black pepper

*1/8 teaspoon cayenne pepper**

¼ cup diced tomatoes in juice**

3 cups Best Homemade Chicken Stock (see recipe page 36) or store-bought

1 corn tortilla (one left over from a previous recipe works best)***

Pinch of salt

1 tablespoon chopped fresh cilantro (optional)

2 tablespoons shredded cheese, such as Cotija, cheddar, or Monterey Jack (optional)

1 green onion, sliced thin on an angle (optional)

Heat a medium saucepan over medium-high heat. When it's warm, add the vegetable oil and wait 30 seconds. Add the onions and celery and sauté for a couple of minutes, until they start looking translucent. Add the garlic and sauté for another minute; stirring the mixture frequently so the garlic doesn't burn. Add the chicken, followed by the *Flavor Blast!* ingredients (the cumin, paprika, oregano, black pepper, and cayenne pepper); sautéing until fragrant.**** When it smells fragrant, add the tomatoes, stock, and corn tortilla (if you're going to cook the tortilla into the soup; see note). Reduce the heat to medium and let the soup simmer for about 20 minutes, stirring occasionally.

Taste and add salt if needed.

To serve, ladle the soup into bowls and top with cilantro, cheese, green onions, and fried tortilla strips (if using; see note).

Notes From Within Recipe

*You could substitute ½ to 1 whole hot pepper such as jalapeño or serrano for the cayenne. If you want more flavor than heat, remove the seeds and membranes; that's where the serious heat is found.

Using toasted dry chilies such as New Mexican or ancho will add a real complexity to the soup that you just can't get from a ground chili. Toast them without their seeds or stems in a dry skillet over medium heat for about 1 minute, or until fragrant. Then put them in a bowl, cover them with hot water, and let them rehydrate for 30 minutes before chopping them and adding them to the soup. See the video on our blog for a lesson on toasting dry chilies: (*http://karenandcaroleverybite.wordpress.com*).
When handling any hot pepper, use gloves or wash your hands very well after touching it.

** If you'll be using fresh tomatoes, it's nice to peel them first (they're a little more palate-pleasing without the rolled-up, cooked skins), which doesn't take much extra time. Make an X across the bottom of the tomatoes with a paring knife, and then plunge them into boiling water for 30 seconds, or just until the skin just starts to curl up. Remove them and let them cool for a few moments; the peel will easily come off with a paring knife. See our video post on the blog (*http://karenandcaroleverybite.wordpress.com*) for a how-to on peeling tomatoes.

If using canned tomatoes, purchase a 15-ounce can, and freeze the remainder for later use.

***There are several schools of thought on how to use tortillas when making soup. Some folks use them as a thickener to make a very hearty soup. Others prefer the tortilla cut into strips, and then fried in oil until crispy and served on top of the soup. While others just crumble corn chips on top.
If you want to fry your tortilla, just cut it into thin strips, heat about ¼ cup of vegetable oil in a small pan, and fry a few of the strips until they have turned a little dark and are crispy. Drain them well on a paper towel and season them with a pinch of salt.

****This helps release the volatile oils in the dry spices, which is important in flavoring the whole dish.

Recipe Notes

_____

_____

_____

_____

_____

_____

_____

_____

_____

_____

_____

_____

_____

_____

Chapter 2

Calling All Fowl: Gobble, Gobble **Turkey**!

Herb-Roasted Turkey Breast with Tomatoes and Cauliflower

Yield: 1 to 2 servings

Turkey is a great meat any time of the year, not just Thanksgiving! This is a delicious, fail-safe recipe. Baby Kale Salad with White Beans and Mustard Vinaigrette (pages 139) would pair nicely with this.

2 tablespoons butter, softened

Flavor Blast!
1 tablespoon minced fresh Italian parsley, or 1 teaspoon dried
2 teaspoons minced garlic
2 teaspoons dried sage
½ teaspoon freshly ground black pepper
1 teaspoon salt

1 (2-pound) turkey breast, bone in and skin on
1 small onion, cut into ½-inch chunks (1 cup)
2 large carrots, sliced ¼-inch thick (1 cup)
1 cup frozen cauliflower flowerets, thawed*
5 fresh plum tomatoes, halved
2 tablespoons olive oil
Salt and freshly ground pepper

Preheat the oven to 375°F.

Put the butter in a small bowl and add the *Flavor Blast!* ingredients (the Italian parsley, garlic, sage, black pepper, and salt). Using a fork, mash and thoroughly stir the butter together until everything is evenly distributed.

Pat the turkey dry with paper towels. **Do not rinse** it, as this can contaminate your sink area with splatter from the water. Gently loosen the skin of the turkey breast by taking your index finger and gently lifting the skin up and away from the meat itself, being careful not to tear the skin. Stuff the herbed butter under the skin and spread it around until all the meat is covered.

In a separate bowl, toss the onions, carrots, cauliflower, and plum tomatoes with the olive oil. Season to taste with salt and pepper until they are evenly coated. Put the vegetables in a large baking dish and lay the turkey breast, skin side up, on top of the vegetables. Coat the turkey skin with some of the seasoned olive oil left in the bottom of the bowl. Bake for about 45 minutes, or until an instant-read meat thermometer inserted into the thickest part of the breast, being careful not to touch bone, reads 160°F. If you don't have a meat thermometer (although we recommend it as they're both inexpensive and a great tool for the kitchen), press the breast slightly after the full 45 minutes, and it should have just a little bit of give. Both the turkey and vegetables should be a rich, golden brown.

Let the turkey rest in the baking dish for at least 10 minutes before slicing. Serve with roasted vegetables** on the side.

NOTE: Save the leftover meat for the other delicious recipes in this chapter (or other recipes you enjoy). The turkey pieces can also be refrigerated for 4–5 days or frozen for a month. You can also make turkey stock (that can be frozen for up to 3 months) with the leftover bones. Making turkey stock is the same as the instructions and guidelines from The Best Homemade Chicken Stock recipe (page 36). Everything will just be in a smaller amount because these are bones from a 2-pound turkey breast, and not a full chicken. But the idea is the same!

Notes From Within Recipe

*It is easier to use frozen cauliflower florets in this recipe because you can easily save the remaining in the freezer for use next time, or in another recipe. If you use fresh, you will have a large head of cauliflower leftover and unless you plan on eating it as a side dish (simply roasting it in the oven is a delicious choice!) or within the next few days with another dinner, you will have a good deal of cauliflower left that could go bad and go to waste. Waste=boo!

Other options to not waste the leftover cauliflower would be to ask your grocer to cut the head in half & sell you only the half you need, share with a neighbor, or blanche and freeze for later use (see the video on our blog about blanching: *http://karenandcaroleverybite.wordpress.com*)

**This recipe includes extra vegetables to use in the Not Thanksgiving Turkey Sandwich and the *Last Bite* recipe in this chapter.

Turkey Salad with Grapes and Gorgonzola

Yield: 1 to 2 servings

This salad is simple, crispy, creamy, and sweet. What could be better?

½ cup shredded Herb-Roasted Turkey Breast (see recipe page 45)
½ cup green grapes, halved
2 tablespoons crumbled Gorgonzola cheese*
1 to 2 tablespoons Balsamic Vinaigrette Dressing (see recipe page 183)
3 cups romaine lettuce, torn into bite-size pieces**
Fresh cracked pepper (optional)

In a large bowl, mix the turkey with the grapes and Gorgonzola. Add the balsamic vinaigrette and lettuce. Mix well and pile onto a chilled plate. Top with pepper, if desired.

Notes From Within Recipe

*You can also use Italian-style Gorgonzola Dolce cheese; it will be quite a bit creamier than regular Gorgonzola but mixes in very nicely. But whatever Gorgonzola you find at the store will be wonderful. It's yummy Gorgonzola after all!

**Use a salad spinner to dry your lettuce or pat it dry with clean kitchen towels. Also, when you cut lettuce with a knife, you slice through its cells and expose them to oxygen, thus causing browning to occur more quickly. The best way to prevent this is to tear the lettuce.

Golden Turkey & Spinach Pastry Pockets with Green Grape Salsa

Yield: 1 to 2 servings

Not only a mouthful to say, but a tasty mouthful that will knock your socks off! Use some of your remaining turkey for these tasty pastry pockets. The green grape salsa adds a little tart freshness to brighten things up!

1 teaspoon butter

2 cups fresh spinach (or 5oz of frozen spinach thawed and squeezed dry)

½ cup shredded Herb-Roasted Turkey Breast (see recipe page 45)

2 tablespoons crumbled Gorgonzola cheese

½ recipe Herbed Pastry (see recipe within Fabulous Flaky Pie Crust recipe, page 198)*

For the salsa:
1 cup minced green grapes

Flavor Blast!
1 tablespoon minced green onion, both white and green parts
2 teaspoons minced fresh Italian parsley
1 teaspoon minced fresh rosemary

2 teaspoons freshly squeezed lemon juice

1 tablespoon olive oil

2 tablespoons walnuts, toasted and chopped (optional)**

Milk or water, for brushing the pastry

Toasted walnuts (optional)

Preheat the oven to 400°F.

Heat a medium sauté pan over medium-high heat and add the butter. Cook the butter until it foams and browns slightly; stirring and turning down the heat if necessary so it doesn't burn. Add the spinach and sauté for 1 to 2 minutes, or until it's just wilted. Remove from the heat, and let it cool for 5 to 10 minutes. When the spinach is cool enough to handle, squeeze it to remove the moisture.***

Roughly chop the spinach and put it in a medium bowl. Add the turkey breast and Gorgonzola and mix very well.

Roll out the crust into two 6 to 7-inch circles. Place half the filling mixture in one circle and half in the other, being sure to leave about a ½-inch border around the edge (to allow room for folding it over). Lightly brush the pastry with milk or water around the ½-inch border. Fold the pastry over the filling into a half-moon shape, and press down all around the edges to make sure they're thoroughly sealed.

Next, crimp the edges with a fork or your fingers this to complete the seal and make pretty indentations.
(See our blog post at *http://karenandcaroleverybite.wordpress.com* about making pastry pockets and crimping the edges.)

Place the pockets on a parchment paper or Silpat-lined baking sheet. Brush the top of each pocket lightly with milk to help it brown. Cut three ½-inch slits in the top of each pocket to allow steam to escape. Bake at 400°F for about 30 minutes, or until they're golden brown. Let them cool for 5 minutes before serving—the insides of the pockets will be piping hot!

While the pastry pockets are baking, make the green grape salsa.

In a small bowl, mix the grapes with the *Flavor Blast!* ingredients (the green onion, parsley, and rosemary). Add the lemon juice and olive oil, and mix well. Let sit for a few minutes to allow all the flavors to come together.

To serve, spoon the salsa on top of the hot pastry pockets and sprinkle with the toasted walnuts, if desired.

Notes From Within Recipe

*Since you're only using half of the Herbed Pastry recipe, you can either make a half-recipe now, or make a full recipe and freeze the other half. The pastry will keep in the freezer for up to a month.

**Toasting walnuts (or any nut) is easy peasy. Place the nuts in a pie pan, on a piece of aluminum foil, or an ovenproof sauté pan. Bake in a preheated 400°F oven about 5 to 7 minutes, or until lightly browned. You can also toast them in a sauté pan on the stove. Heat the nuts for about 5 minutes over medium heat. Whether you're toasting in the oven or on the stove, but sure to keep an eye on them! They can go from "barely toasted" to "burnt" in record time!

***If you don't squeeze the liquid out of the spinach, it will make the pastry very soggy and wet. Yuck!

Not Thanksgiving Turkey Sandwich

Yield: 1 sandwich

The perfect turkey sandwich that doesn't rely on holidays, gravy, or a nap.

1 roasted tomato half from Herb-Roasted Turkey Breast (see recipe, page 45), finely chopped .

1 tablespoon roasted onion from Herb-Roasted Turkey Breast (see recipe, page 45), finely chopped

½ tablespoon Balsamic Vinaigrette Dressing (see recipe page 183)

1 tablespoon mayonnaise

Salt and freshly ground pepper

2 slices artisan bread, lightly toasted*

4 ounces sliced Herb-Roasted Turkey Breast (see recipe page 45)

2 large romaine lettuce leaves

Drizzle of Extra-Virgin Olive Oil

In a small bowl, mix the tomatoes, onions, balsamic dressing, and mayonnaise together. Taste for seasoning and add salt and pepper if needed. Smear half of the mayonnaise mixture onto each half of the bread, pile on the turkey and romaine, and top with the other half of the bread. Cut the sandwich in half and eat with wild abandon!

Note From Within Recipe

*Use extra bread to make homemade croutons or bread pudding, or grab a couple of nice firm apples and make a Brown Betty.

Last Bite Recipe: Shredded Turkey with Herbed Basmati Rice

Yield: 1 serving

A *Last Bite* recipe that uses up any odds and ends for a satisfying meal.

2 teaspoons olive oil

1 teaspoon minced garlic

2 teaspoons minced fresh Italian parsley

¾ cup vegetables from Herb-Roasted Turkey Breast (see recipe, page 45), cut into ¼-inch dice (or as close to 1 cup as you have left over)

½ cup uncooked basmati or other fragrant rice such as Thai jasmine *

1 cup The Best Homemade Chicken Stock (see recipe, page 36), or use pan juices left over from Herb-Roasted Turkey Breast added together with water to make 1 cup

½ cup shredded Herb-Roasted Turkey Breast (see recipe, page 54)

Flavor Blast!
1 teaspoon minced fresh Italian parsley
¼ teaspoon finely grated lemon zest (yellow rind only; none of the white pith)
1/8 teaspoon salt
Freshly ground pepper to taste

Heat a large saucepan over medium-high heat for 1 minute. Add the olive oil and heat for an additional 30 seconds. When the oil is hot, add the garlic and parsley and sauté for about 2 minutes, or until the garlic is just starting to brown. Add the vegetables and sauté 2 minutes more, or until they're thoroughly warmed through. When the vegetables are warm, add the rice, stir well, and sauté for 2 to 3 minutes. This allows the rice to toast slightly and adds depth of flavor. Add the chicken stock, bring it to a boil for 15 seconds, reduce the heat to low, and cover the pan with a tight-fitting lid. Cook for about 20 minutes.

When the rice has cooked for 20 minutes, turn the heat off, remove the lid, add the shredded turkey, and mix well with the rice and vegetables. Cover and let the food rest off the burner for 5 minutes to finish cooking and heat the turkey. Meanwhile, in a small bowl, mix the *Flavor Blast!* ingredients (the Italian parsley, lemon zest, salt, and pepper) together. Sprinkle them on top of the turkey and rice just before serving.

Note From Within Recipe

*If you have some already cooked rice leftover from another recipe, you can certainly use that here. Simply add in the rice to the pan after the vegetables have been added in and warmed.

Recipe Notes

Chapter 3

Dinner from the Hoof: **Beef** and **Pork**

This chapter is split up into two "hoof" sections: *Beef* and *Pork*.

Section 1: Beef

Succulent Braised Pot Roast with Root Vegetables

Yield: 1 pot roast with plenty of leftovers for other recipes!

One of the loveliest comfort foods is a tender braised chuck roast with vegetables in a rich broth, aka pot roast. It's baked in a "pot," thus the name.

1 (3-pound) chuck roast

1 tablespoon salt

1½ teaspoons freshly ground black pepper

2 tablespoons vegetable oil, divided

1 small onion (about the size of a baseball or peach), cut into ½-inch dice (1 cup)

1 stalk celery, cut into ½-inch dice (½ cup)

6 to 8 cloves garlic, smashed flat as a piece of paper

2 tablespoons minced fresh Italian parsley

½ cup red wine, drinking quality only (optional to have the wine, but not optional to have low quality wine. You always want to cook with wine that you drink!)

1 (15-ounce) can diced tomatoes in juice

1-inch-wide strip lemon zest

3 cups vegetables (any of the following: onion, celery, carrots, parsnips, or potatoes), cut into ½-inch dice

Preheat the oven to 350°F.

Season the chuck roast all over with the salt and pepper, rubbing it into the meat well (don't be shy). Heat a skillet, Dutch oven, or other ovenproof pan large enough to hold the roast without crowding over medium-high heat. When the skillet is hot, add 1 tablespoon of the oil; wait 30 seconds and then add the roast. You should hear the meat searing; if you don't, remove the roast and wait a moment or two for the oil to heat up before putting it back in.* Sear the meat until it's nicely browned on all sides. Remove the meat to a plate and discard any remaining oil.

Add the remaining 1 tablespoon of oil to the skillet, along with the onion, celery, and garlic. Sauté until the onion is translucent, about 3 to 4 minutes. Add the parsley and sauté for an additional minute. Add the wine and stir; using the addition of the wine to help you scrape up those flavor bits that have stuck to the bottom of the pan.** Let everything simmer together until the wine has reduced down to half the original amount; about 5 minutes. Finally, add the tomatoes, lemon zest, and a dash of salt and pepper.

Return the roast to the pan and cover it with the vegetables. Cover the pan with parchment paper and cover that with aluminum foil (the parchment stops the tomatoes from reacting with the foil). Braise the roast in the oven for about 2½ to 3 hours, or until it's fork-tender.***

Serve the roast along with the cooked vegetables with a nice side salad and some good, crusty, artisan bread.

Be sure to save the leftover sauce, along with the meat and vegetables; you'll need it for the other recipes in this chapter!

Notes From Within Recipe

*There are two secrets behind making a great pot roast: 1) creating a hard sear on the meat to seal in the flavor, followed by 2) cooking the meat at a low temperature in a little liquid in a well-sealed pot. This is called braising. Braising makes a tough cut tender, and the fat found in these inexpensive cuts make the meat extra delicious.

**This scraping up of the browned bits at the bottom of the pan with the addition of a liquid (wine, water, or stock) is called deglazing and aids in making a very flavorful overall dish.

***Fork-tender means that when you stick a fork into the food, the food pulls away easily.

Beef Potpie with Thyme and Garlic Crust

Yield: 1 to 2 servings

Potpie is the quintessential comfort food: it's easy to make, easy to eat, and it always pleases.

1 cup roughly chopped Succulent Braised Pot Roast (page 61), including vegetables and sauce
¼ cup peas, fresh or frozen and thawed
¼ cup corn kernels, fresh or frozen and thawed

Flavor Blast!
1 teaspoon minced fresh thyme
1 teaspoon minced garlic
¼ teaspoon freshly ground black pepper

½ recipe Herbed Pie Crust section of the Fabulous Flaky Pie Crust recipe (see recipe, page 198)
Milk, for brushing the pastry

Preheat the oven to 400°F.

In a large bowl, mix the pot roast, vegetables, sauce, peas, and corn. Set aside.

Gently knead the *Flavor Blast!* ingredients (the thyme, garlic, and black pepper) into the herbed pie crust pastry. On a lightly floured surface, roll the pastry out to 1/8 inch thick. Cut out 2 circles; one will be the bottom of the potpie and one the top—the top one should be a bit larger than the top by about 3 inches: the size will depend on the size of your baking dish or pie pan. Lay the larger circle across a small pie pan or ovenproof baking dish, leaving about a ½-inch overhang.

Fill the pastry with the meat mixture, and then top with the smaller circle. Fold the bottom edge over the top one and pinch the edges together with your thumb and index finger so the filling doesn't bubble out the sides when you bake it.

Cut a steam hole in the top and brush the pastry with a little milk to encourage browning.

Bake the potpie for about 30 to 40 minutes, or until its golden brown. Let it rest for 5 to 8 minutes before eating.

Variation: This recipe could easily be made into a pastry pocket: see either the Chicken Stuffed Pastry Pocket recipe on page 35 or the Golden Turkey & Spinach Pastry Pockets with Green Grape Salsa recipe on page 50 for the technique. Also, just use one top crust if you are trying to cut down on carbs.

French Dip Sandwich with a Hearty Jus

Yield: 1 to 2 servings

The simplest of meals and one of the most satisfying sandwiches: shredded, braised meat, drenched in roasted vegetables and sauce from the pot roast, and piled high on a toasted roll.

1 (6-inch) French roll, split lengthwise and lightly toasted*
4 ounces Succulent Braised Pot Roast (page 61), sliced or shredded and warmed
½ cup vegetables from Succulent Braised Pot Roast (page 61), warmed
Leftover sauce from the Succulient Braised Pot Roast (page 61)

Put the braised beef on the roll, then top with the vegetables and some of the sauce. Pour the rest of the sauce into a bowl and dunk the sandwich as desired. Serve immediately.

Note From Within Recipe

*If you have leftover French rolls, toast them and shred finely to make breadcrumbs.

Last Bite Recipe: Beef Barley Soup with "Sopper" Bread

Yield: 1 to 2 servings

Beef Barley is such a hearty, rich soup. It really will warm you from the inside out! "Sopper" bread is our term to "sop" up all that rich broth with some good, crusty bread!

1 tablespoon olive oil
2 tablespoons finely diced onion
1 tablespoon finely diced celery
1 tablespoon finely diced carrot
2 cremini or brown mushrooms, sliced into ¼-inch pieces*

Flavor Blast!
1 tablespoon minced fresh Italian parsley
1 large clove garlic, smashed flat as a piece of paper

¼ cup red wine, drinking quality only, or water

½ cup shredded Succulent Braised Pot Roast (see recipe, page 61), including any leftover vegetables and sauce

¼ cup pearl barley

2 cups Best Homemade Chicken Stock (see recipe page 36) or water

Salt and freshly ground pepper

1 recipe "Sopper" Bread (see recipe, page 83)

Heat a large saucepan over medium-high heat for about 30 seconds to 1 minute. Add the olive oil, and wait for an additional 30 seconds. Add the onions, celery, carrots, and mushrooms, and sauté until the onions are translucent; about 4 minutes. Add the *Flavor Blast!* ingredients (the Italian parsley and garlic) and sauté for 2 minutes.

Deglaze the pan with the wine and let the liquid reduce until it's almost gone (this really concentrates the flavors). Add the roast, leftover vegetables, and sauce, and the barley. Stir well and add the chicken stock.

Reduce the heat to a low simmer and let the soup cook for about 40 minutes, stirring occasionally, or until the barley is tender. Season to taste with salt and pepper.

Serve with "sopper" bread.

Notes From Within Recipe

*Grocery stores most often times have mushrooms in bulk, so you can just buy a few at the time. If they do not, and you have to purchase a larger package, simply slice and sauté them up in a little butter. They make a great addition to any recipe in this chapter!

Brown mushrooms generally have more flavor than white mushrooms. Just remember: brown=extra flavor!

Section 2: Pork

Simply Tasty Pork Shoulder with Root Vegetables

Yield: 1 pork roast with plenty of leftovers

This is one of those foundation recipes that should be in everyone's repertoire.
A true tasty delight!

For the pork:
1 (3-pound) pork shoulder, bone-in if possible*
1 tablespoon olive oil

Flavor Blast!
2 tablespoons salt
½ tablespoon black pepper
10 cloves garlic, smashed flat as a piece of paper
2 tablespoons minced fresh Italian parsley, or 1 tablespoon dried

For the vegetables:
3 cups vegetables (any of the following: onion, celery, carrots,
parsnips, potatoes, or fennel bulb**) cut into ½-inch dice
2 tablespoons olive oil
½ tablespoon salt
1 teaspoon black pepper

In a large bowl or on a cutting board, season the pork shoulder with the *Flavor Blast!* ingredients (the salt, black pepper, garlic, and Italian parsley) by rubbing them on the meat and coating the surface evenly.***

Put the pork on a cooling rack and then place the rack on a sheet pan. Doing this will allow any juices to drip away and, along with the salt, will keep the roast nice and dry to seal in the flavor.
Leave the roast <u>uncovered </u>in the fridge overnight.****

Next day: preheat the oven to 350°F.

When you're ready to cook the pork, heat a large skillet over medium-high heat. When the skillet is hot, add the olive oil and heat it for 30 seconds. Add the pork and brown it well on all sides; this will take several minutes for each side. You want a nice brown crust all around.

While the pork is browning, toss the vegetables in the oil, salt, and pepper until they're evenly coated. Place one quarter of the vegetables in the bottom of a baking dish that is large enough to hold the pork and vegetables without overcrowding. Reserve the rest of the vegetables, as you will bake them during the last 30 minutes of the pork cooking.

When the pork is well browned, place it on top of the vegetables in the baking dish. Discard any oil remaining in the skillet and add ½ cup of cold water to the pan, scraping up all the browned bits on the pan bottom.***** Cover the roast and vegetables with parchment paper, then cover that with aluminum foil (if you only have foil, make sure it's not touching the roast so the two don't react together while baking).

The pork will need to bake for about 2 hours, or until the meat is fork-tender. About ½ an hour before the pork is done, spread the reserved vegetables on a sheet pan and bake for about 30 minutes, or until they're soft to the touch.

Remove the pan from the oven and let the meat rest. While the vegetables finishing up in the oven, remove the pork to a plate. Create a "sauce" by using a hand blender to puree the vegetables that cooked with the roast (or smash them up with a fork).

To Serve

If the roast is truly fork tender, pull pieces apart with a fork, spoon the "sauce" over the top and serve the roasted vegetables on the side.

If the roast is not quite fork tender and you do need to slice it, be sure to slice the pork against the grain.

> NOTE: You always want to cut meat against the grain (the grain describes the fibers within the meat itself, which all go in one direction.) Cutting this way gives you short, tender strands, as opposed to cutting with the grain, which will give you long, stringy, tough fibers.

Spoon the sauce over the top and serve the roasted vegetables on the side.

Notes From Within Recipe

*Boneless will also work fine and taste delicious, but a bone-in roast is a little bit better because the bone actually helps flavor the meat as it's cooking, so you get an even richer flavor.

**Fennel bulb has a sweet, mild licorice flavor, but if you don't like licorice, simply leave it out of the recipe.

***We call for a good amount of salt, but it's OK—just rub it all on there! The roast won't taste salty when you eat it, and the salt helps create a nice crust when you sear the meat the next day. We're basically brining the meat, which helps give it a terrific flavor in the end.

****It's OK if you can't prep the night before. Just season the roast as soon as you can—the longer you have the seasonings on there, the better. Pork roast is a cut of meat that is inexpensive, yet packs a lot of flavor. The secret to getting even more flavor is to season it ahead of the actual cooking as much as possible. So while overnight isn't crucial to making the roast, the extra time it sits to soak up all those flavors inside and out will just make it even better.

Also, with these less expensive cuts of meat, you generally need slower and longer cooking times to draw out all of their amazing flavor.

The reason you leave the pork uncovered is to help dry out the meat. Meat that has been a bit dried out tends to brown better, and a tasty, nicely-seared crust is what we're looking for! It's kept in the refrigerator, so it will be kept cool, and thus will be fine and safe to use and eat.

*****You could use a splash of red or white wine instead of water to deglaze the pan. If you use a nonstick skillet, no pork will stick to the pan bottom, so there will be no need to deglaze. Either type of skillet will work fine. Just use whatever you have.

Asian-Style Pork Baguettes with Carrot Slaw

Yield: 2 servings

These baguettes are salty, spicy, crunchy, and sweet. A lot of great flavors and different textures going on here!

For the pork:

Flavor Blast!
1 teaspoon finely minced or grated fresh ginger
1 teaspoon finely minced or grated garlic
2 tablespoons minced green onion, both white and green parts

1 tablespoon soy sauce
2 teaspoons sesame oil (either light or dark toasted)
1 cup shredded Simply Tasty Pork Shoulder (see recipe page 71)

For the slaw:
¼ cup sliced or shredded radish
¼ cup shredded carrot
2 teaspoons jalapeno pepper; sliced thin (remove seeds and membranes for less heat)
2–3 sprigs fresh cilantro, roughly torn (or use some frozen minced that you previously saved)*
2 tablespoons rice wine vinegar or other vinegar**
1 teaspoon sugar

2 French rolls or baguette

To make the pork: in a medium bowl, mix the *Flavor Blast!* ingredients (the ginger, garlic, and green onion), soy sauce, and sesame oil. Let the sauce sit while you get the pork ready, so the flavors have a chance to blend together.

Slice the pork into ¼-inch thick pieces and warm in a sauté pan over medium heat, and add the sauce when the meat is warmed through; about 4 minutes.

To make the slaw: in another medium bowl, mix the carrot, radish, jalapeño, cilantro, and vinegar. Start by adding 1 teaspoon of sugar and stir until it dissolves. Taste and adjust the seasoning; add more sugar or vinegar depending on whether you like your slaw sweet or tart.

To assemble the sandwich, lightly toast the buns under the broiler or in a toaster oven, then pile on the pork and top with the slaw.

Notes From Within Recipe

*What to do with leftover cilantro? Adding it to scrambled eggs, potato salad, or a green salad will provide a great *Flavor Blast!*
Or substitute it for basil in your favorite pesto recipe. Puree with a touch of oil and freeze in small quantities to add to soups, or salsas at the drop of a hat.

**Rice wine vinegar is a little sweeter than other vinegars, but you don't have to use it. Experiment with what you have. And if you don't have any vinegar on hand, use lemon or lime juice (2 tablespoons as well) and adjust to taste.

Pork Tacos with Roasted Chilies

Yield: 2 servings

Kick beef tacos to the curb and try these pork tacos for dinner. They would make a taco truck proud!

This dish pairs nicely with Pleasing Pinto Beans (see recipe, page 155) and Heavenly Herbed Rice (see recipe, page 155).

2 teaspoons vegetable oil

Flavor Blast!
1 teaspoon minced garlic
½ teaspoon ground cumin
½ teaspoon sweet paprika
¼ teaspoon dried oregano

2 tablespoons diced roasted chili peppers, fresh* or canned
¼ cup diced tomatoes in juice**
1 cup shredded Simply Tasty Pork Shoulder (recipe page 71)
4 corn or flour tortillas
2 to 3 sprigs fresh cilantro (optional)

Heat a medium skillet over medium-high heat. When the skillet is hot, add the oil and wait 30 seconds. Add the garlic and sauté until it's just barely starting to brown, and then add the rest of the *Flavor Blast!* ingredients (the cumin, paprika, and oregano) and sauté for a minute, or until the spices are fragrant.*** Add the chilies, tomatoes, and pork, and sauté until the sauce is slightly reduced, about 5 minutes.

Heat another skillet over high heat and warm the tortillas one at a time, spooning the pork filling into each as they come out of the skillet. Top with the fresh cilantro.****

NOTE: For a delicious gluten-free option, toss the pork filling with shredded lettuce and sliced avocado with Basic Vinaigrette (see recipe, page 197).

Notes From Within Recipe

*Use fresh poblanos or banana peppers if you want some mild spice or bell peppers for no spice. To roast them, simply blacken the skin by putting the pepper directly on the flame of a gas burner or under the broiler and then turning it as the skin blisters. (If you're roasting hot peppers on a burner, don't keep your face over them, as you may roast your sinuses instead!) When the peppers are blackened, put them in a bowl and cover it with a plate, lid, or plastic wrap. Let the peppers cool for about 15 minutes. When they're cool enough to handle, peel the skin off; remove the core, stem, and seeds; and cut them into small dice.

**Since you're not using the whole can, you can freeze the remainder and use it later instead of fresh tomatoes in our Pleasing Pinto Beans recipe (page 155). You can also freeze for a later use.

***When you cook with spices, we recommend heating them first to bring out their volatile oils.

****If using cilantro that you've frozen, make sure it has been thawed out and dried off before using. See our discussion in "Prepping Ahead", and the videos on our blog: *http://karenandcaroleverybite.wordpress.com*, on freezing herbs and blanching.

Last Bite Recipe: Pork and White Bean Soup with "Sopper" Bread

Yield: 1 to 2 servings

This soup is hearty and filling. Definitely a tasty and different way to enjoy that leftover pork roast!

1 tablespoon olive oil
2 tablespoons finely diced onion
1 tablespoon finely diced celery*
Flavor Blast!
1 clove garlic, smashed flat as a piece of paper
½ teaspoon dried oregano

½ cup finely seeded and diced fresh tomato
½ cup shredded Simply Tasty Pork Shoulder-only the pork (see recipe page 71)
½ (15-ounce) can of white beans, such as cannellini, navy or small white beans **
2 cups Best Homemade Chicken Stock (see recipe page 36) or water
Salt and freshly ground pepper
½ teaspoon freshly ground black pepper
1 bay leaf
2 sprigs fresh Italian parsley (or other leftover herb from a previous recipe)

1 recipe "Sopper" Bread (recipe follows)

Heat a large saucepan over medium-high heat for 1 minute. Add the olive oil and wait for 30 seconds. Add the onions and celery and sauté until translucent, about 4 minutes. Add the *Flavor Blast!* ingredients (the garlic and oregano) and cook for an additional minute. Add the tomato, pork, beans, and the chicken stock or water.

Reduce the heat to low and simmer the soup for about 15 minutes. Season to taste with salt and pepper. Serve with sopper bread and a salad, if desired.

Notes From Within Recipe

*If you don't have any celery on hand, it's okay to leave out in this recipe.
If you do buy one bunch of celery and have a lot leftover, freeze it and use it to make stock, or take it as a snack to work with a little hummus or peanut butter.

Here is a quick and easy recipe suggestion for any extra celery you have:

"Braised Celery"
Cut the celery stalks into 3–4 inch sticks. Heat a small amount (maybe a ¼-inch pat) or some leftover bacon fat in a sauté pan until hot. Add in the celery stalks and sauté for about 5–6 minutes. Add in some extra diced onions and/or tomatoes you have from a previous recipe, and stir. Place a lid on the pan, reduce the heat to low, and cook for about 30 minutes; or until tender and tasty.

**If you're using canned beans, be sure to rinse them gently but well.
Use the extra ½ can of beans to make a scrumptious spread: mash them in a bowl with a drizzle of olive oil, 1 teaspoon each of minced garlic and fresh Italian parsley, and salt and pepper to taste. Spoon onto toasted bread and top with minced tomatoes. Yum!

"Sopper" Bread

Yield: 1 slice
(ingredients can be easily adjusted as needed)

This bread is tasty on its own, but you can certainly use it to sop up all the yumminess from the above recipes!

1 thick slice hearty country-style bread
1 garlic clove
Olive oil for drizzling
Parmesan cheese

Toast the bread in a toaster or under a broiler. Rub the warm bread with the garlic, drizzle to taste with the olive oil, and top with the Parmesan. Briefly broil the bread until the cheese has melted.

Recipe Notes

Chapter 4

Jazzing Up the Daily Grind:
Ground Beef

Not Your Mom's Meatloaf

Yield: 1 large loaf

That's right: meatloaf schmeatloaf (Carol's favorite movie)!

This one is tender, juicy, and full of flavor. Serve it with a Castaway Salad (see recipe, page 184) and/or Balsamic-Glazed Carrots (see recipe page 159).

½ cup minced onions
¼ cup minced celery
2 tablespoons minced garlic
3 tablespoons minced sun-dried tomatoes

Flavor Blast!
2 tablespoons minced fresh Italian parsley
1 tablespoon dried basil
1 teaspoon dried oregano
2 teaspoons salt
1½ teaspoons freshly ground black pepper

2 tablespoons soy sauce or tamari sauce

1 egg

½ cup bread crumbs, crushed crackers, or Panko breadcrumbs, or gluten-free breadcrumbs*

1 pound ground pork

1 pound ground turkey

½ pound ground beef

Preheat the oven to 350°F.

In a large bowl, mix the onions, celery, garlic, sun-dried tomatoes, *Flavor Blast!* ingredients (the parsley, basil, oregano, salt and pepper), soy sauce, eggs, and bread crumbs. Crumble the ground pork, turkey, and beef over the top and gently mix everything together, using a light hand.** Form the mixture into a loaf shape (roughly 2½ inches thick by 6 to 7 inches long by 3 inches wide). Place the meatloaf in a baking dish, pie pan, or loaf pan. Whatever you have on hand that will hold the loaf!

Bake for about 30 minutes, or until an instant-read meat thermometer inserted into the middle reads 160°F. Let the meatloaf rest for at least 8 minutes before slicing. Brush any juices from the pan over the sliced meatloaf and serve.

Notes From Within Recipe

*Panko breadcrumbs are a Japanese style breadcrumb. It's a very light breadcrumb that makes for great breading. Try them with your best oven fried chicken recipe (or deep fried for that matter) or any other time you use breadcrumbs.

**You want to stir with a light hand so you don't make the texture too tough by over-mixing or mixing too vigorously.

Fried Meatloaf Bites (aka Meatloaf Meatballs!) with Linguini

Yield: 1 to 2 servings

What could better than crispy bits of meatloaf goodness in a zippy tomato sauce served over yummy pasta? Not much, we think!

1 tablespoon olive oil

1 cup (about 4 ounces) ½-inch chunks of Not Your Mom's Meatloaf (see recipe page 86)

1½ cups Zippy Tomato Sauce (see recipe page 196), or use a good canned variety

2 ounces dried linguini

1 tablespoon grated Parmesan cheese, or more to taste

1 teaspoon finely chopped parsley (optional)

Heat a small sauté pan over medium-high heat. Add the oil and then wait 30 seconds. Add the meatloaf chunks, browning them well on each side, for a total of about 5 to 6 minutes.

While the meatloaf browns, prepare the tomato sauce and linguini. To do so, first thoroughly warm the tomato sauce in a small saucepan. For the linguini, bring 2 quarts of water plus 1 tablespoon of salt to a boil. Add the linguini and cook for about 8 minutes, stirring often. Drain it well and then toss it with the hot tomato sauce.* Pile the pasta on a plate and top with the crispy meatloaf chunks, Parmesan, and parsley (if desired).**

Notes From Within Recipe

*The secret to a great pasta dish is to let the drained pasta sit in your sauce for a few minutes. It really helps the flavors come together nicely.

**For a delicious gluten-free option, enjoy the meatloaf bites on a tasty dinner salad. Prepare a salad with any and all the fixings you like, then top with the meatloaf bites, your favorite dressing, and some Parmesan cheese.

Easy Stuffed Peppers with Meatloaf, Corn, and Cheese

Yield: 1 to 2 servings

These Easy Stuffed Peppers are a great way to use some odds and ends for a really satisfying meal. Serve them with a side salad to bump up your veggie intake.

1 large red, yellow, or orange bell pepper

½ cup crumbled Not Your Mom's Meatloaf (see recipe page 86)

½ cup Heavenly Herbed Rice (see recipe page 155), or other leftover rice from a previous recipe

¼ cup corn kernels, fresh or frozen and thawed

½ cup Zippy Tomato Sauce (see recipe, page 196) or use a good canned variety

2 tablespoons shredded cheddar cheese

Preheat the oven to 375°F.

Halve the pepper, lengthwise, and remove the seeds and any membranes.

In a medium bowl, thoroughly mix the meatloaf with the rice, corn, and tomato sauce. Stuff half of the mixture into each pepper half. Top each with 1 tablespoon of the cheddar. Place the peppers on a small baking sheet or in a baking dish that holds the peppers without crowding them. Bake them for about 20 to 25 minutes, or until the filling is hot and bubbly and the pepper is fork-tender.

Serve immediately for best flavor!

Tasty Tacos with Tomato Salsa and Cilantro Pesto

Yield: 1 to 2 servings

Mmm, tacos—everyone's favorite! Serve these for a quick lunch or with Pleasing Pinto Beans (page 155) and Heavenly Herbed Rice (page 155) for dinner.

For the salsa:

Flavor Blast!
1 teaspoon minced garlic
1 tablespoon freshly squeezed lime juice
½ teaspoon ground cumin
1 tablespoon minced onion (or use red onion to add a touch of sweetness)

¼ cup minced tomatoes
2 teaspoons olive oil
Salt and freshly ground pepper
For the pesto:
2 teaspoons minced garlic
½ cup fresh cilantro
2 tablespoons almonds or cashews
1 tablespoon Greek-style plain yogurt*
Pinch of salt and freshly ground pepper

For the tacos:
2 teaspoons olive oil
½ cup crumbled Not Your Mom's Meatloaf (see recipe page 86)
3–4 corn or flour tortillas
½ cup shredded lettuce

To make the salsa: in a small bowl, mix the *Flavor Blast!* ingredients (the garlic, lime juice, cumin, and onion). Add the tomatoes and olive oil. Mix well and season to taste with salt and pepper. Set the salsa aside while you make the pesto.

To make the pesto**: coat the garlic, cilantro, and almonds with a few drops of the yogurt and begin grinding them into a rough paste using a mortar and pestle.*** Add the rest of the yogurt and continue to grind. When the pesto has reached a creamy consistency, season to taste with salt and pepper; it will have a nutty tart flavor. Another option is to make the pesto in a small food chopper or food processor. If using a chopper or processor, mix all the ingredients except the yogurt and pulse a few times to achieve a rough consistency. Add the yogurt and pulse a few times more. You want the pesto to still have some texture. You're making a pesto not a puree! Set the pesto aside while you make the tacos.

To make the tacos: in a medium skillet on medium high heat, add in the olive oil, and heat for one minute. Add the meatloaf and cook; rotating the pieces around to heat through and to get a crunchy crust formed on all sides.

Heat another skillet on medium-high heat. Add the tortillas one at the time to warm. As each one is warm, remove from pan, and fill with meat, salsa, pesto, and lettuce.

Notes From Within Recipe

*You can make the chicken salad from chapter 1 and keep the leftover yogurt for use in this recipe. If not, just buy a small container and you can enjoy the leftover yogurt with some granola for breakfast.

**Pesto simply refers to the method of preparation (from the Italian *pestare*, to pound or crush), so it can be made out of just about any herb.

***If you don't have a mortar and pestle (or a food chopper or food processor), you can use a medium bowl and the rounded end of a large wooden spoon or any other utensil you can find. Just use something that will give you good pressure/leverage to really get in there and grind everything together to make the pesto.

Last Bite Recipe: Meatloaf Hash with Poached Egg

Yield: 1 to 2 servings

This is a great way to make something that is greater than the sum of its parts. Add the poached eggs for a more powerful protein punch.

1 tablespoon olive oil

½ cup crumbled Not Your Mom's Meatloaf* (see recipe page 86)

2 tablespoons minced onion

1 medium potato, diced (roughly 1/3 cup)

3 tablespoons finely diced bell pepper

Flavor Blast!
1 tablespoon minced fresh Italian parsley
2 teaspoons minced garlic

¼ cup tomatoes, finely diced**

1 cup chopped greens (lettuce, kale, spinach, arugula, or any combination)

1 or 2 eggs

1 teaspoon white vinegar or a squeeze of lemon juice***

Heat a medium skillet over medium-high heat for 1 minute. Add the olive oil and wait 30 seconds. Add the meatloaf, onions, and potatoes and sauté for about 10 to 12 minutes, or until the potatoes are getting soft and lightly browned. Add the peppers and *Flavor Blast!* ingredients (the Italian parsley and garlic) and sauté for 2 to 3 minutes more. Add the tomatoes and continue to sauté until the hash is a little crispy and all the ingredients are soft. Add the greens at the last moment (stirring gently) so they are still bright green and full of flavor and nutrition.

While the hash is cooking, poach the eggs. In a small saucepan, heat about 1½ cups of water over high heat. When the water boils, add the vinegar or lemon juice, and reduce the heat to a simmer. Right before the hash is ready, swirl the water with a spoon, and gently crack the egg into the swirling water. The swirl will make the whites fold back on themselves and makes a nice, compact poached egg. Poach to desired doneness; about 2 to 3 minutes for soft-cooked. Remove the egg from the water with a slotted spoon, letting any water drip away, and serve on top of the hash.

Notes From Within Recipe

*You can easily substitute ½ cup of Classic Roasted Salmon (page 101) instead of the meatloaf—either way is delicious!

**you can certainly use fresh tomatoes, or use canned tomatoes, and freeze the leftovers for another recipe.

***The acid in the vinegar or lemon juice helps to coagulate the proteins in the egg, making it firm up quicker with a nice shape.

Recipe Notes

_____

_____

_____

_____

_____

_____

_____

_____

_____

_____

_____

_____

_____

_____

_____

_____

Chapter 5

Salmon is King!

Classic Roasted Salmon with Vegetable Salsa

Yield: 1–2 servings, with ample leftovers for salmon cakes, a salad, or even salmon & eggs benedict

A classic recipe with a twist.

A fresh, crisp vegetable salsa on the creamy salmon makes a great combination. Enjoy with an easy salad, or with Heavenly Herbed Rice (see recipe, page 155) and steamed sugar snap peas for an easy summer meal.

For the salsa:*
1 tablespoon minced red onion
1 tablespoon minced celery
1 teaspoon minced garlic
1 tablespoon minced fennel bulb**
2 tablespoons seeded and minced fresh tomatoes
1 tablespoon minced fresh Italian parsley
2 tablespoons olive oil
1 tablespoon freshly squeezed lemon juice
½ teaspoon salt
¼ teaspoon freshly ground black pepper

For the salmon:
2 teaspoons olive oil
1 pound wild salmon fillet—bones removed***

Flavor Blast!
1/8 teaspoon salt
Freshly ground pepper
1 tablespoon minced fennel fronds (the feathery tops of the fennel bulb)

To make the salsa, mix all the ingredients together in a medium bowl. Let the salsa sit for 10 to 15 minutes before starting the salmon so the flavors have a chance to blend together.****

Preheat the oven to 350°F.

Brush a small baking sheet with a tiny bit of the olive oil (so the salmon fillet doesn't stick). Drizzle the remaining olive oil over the salmon fillet and season with the *Flavor Blast!* ingredients (the salt, pepper, and fennel fronds). Bake the salmon for 8 to 12 minutes. You don't want to overcook it, so start testing it for doneness at 8 minutes. Test the fillet by gently pressing your finger in the thickest part; if it's done, the salmon will just barely yield to the pressure. If it's not, it will still be firm, and if it's overcooked it will flake or break easily apart. Remember that when you take it out of the oven, it will continue to cook for at least 2 to 3 minutes, so time the cooking accordingly.

To serve, remove the salmon to a plate, spoon the salsa on top, and enjoy immediately.

Notes From Within Recipe

*Save some of this salsa to have with the Scrumptious Salmon Cakes (see recipe, page 104) for dinner another night!

**Before you mince the fennel bulb, remove the core by cutting the fennel in half lengthwise and then cutting the core out in a triangle shape. Save the remaining fennel bulb and fronds in the vegetable drawer of your refrigerator for up to a week (you can use it in other recipes in this book, along with the leftover salmon). See the blog:
http://www.karenandcaroleverybite.wordpress.com for a quick tutorial on fennel.

***If you don't live on the coast then it's probably best to buy your wild salmon in the freezer section pre portioned. That way you just pull out a portion in the morning and defrost it in the refrigerator. When you get home, it will then be ready to go. Studies have shown that wild salmon is more healthy and nutritious then farm raised and better for the environment.

If you can't get salmon or don't enjoy the flavor or texture use a meaty fillet like halibut, snapper or grouper instead. Don't like fish? No problem! Serve the sauce over chicken, burgers, or use to jazz up rice, quinoa or other grains.

To remove the bones just run your finger along the top 1/3 edge and using needle nosed pliers or study tweezers (only used for pulling bones from fish) grasp the bone and pull firmly. If you don't want to pull the bones, just be careful when you eat the fillet.

**** Often times, we think a sauce or salsa needs something more; something more complex. But all it really needs is time. When all the ingredients have some time to sit and blend together, the flavors really begin to come out. After 5–10 minutes, taste and make any additional adjustments you think might be needed.

Scrumptious Salmon Cakes

Yield: 1–2 servings

Breathe new life into salmon by making it into cakes, then pan sauté and serve with a crisp green salad.

½ cup Classic Roasted Salmon (see recipe, page 101), crumbled

¼ cup mayonnaise

1 teaspoon Dijon mustard

2 teaspoons apple cider vinegar*

1 tablespoon minced onion

1 teaspoon minced garlic

2 teaspoons minced Italian parsley

1 egg

¼ cup Ritz Crackers,** crushed

½ cup Panko breadcrumbs

2 tablespoons vegetable oil

2–3 tablespoons Vegetable Salsa—see previous Classic Roasted Salmon recipe (page 101) for the recipe (optional)

½ recipe Castaway Salad—see recipe page 184 (optional)

In a medium bowl, mix the mayonnaise, Dijon mustard, vinegar, onion, garlic, Italian parsley, egg and crushed crackers together into a paste. Add the crumbled salmon and fold together; being careful not to break up the salmon too much. Form the salmon into 4 cakes about ½ inch thick by 2 inches across. Dip each salmon cake in the panko breadcrumbs; being sure to cover all the cakes. Press gently all around to help the panko stick to the salmon cakes. Reserve to a plate.***

In a small sauté pan heated on medium high heat, add the vegetable oil and let heat 30 seconds more. Add the prepared salmon cakes and sauté until golden brown; about 2–3 minutes per side.

While the salmon cakes are cooking, make the Castaway Salad with Balsamic Vinaigrette (if having).

If you have some of the vegetable salsa left from the previous Classic Salmon recipe and you are using that here, just spoon a tablespoon or two onto each hot salmon cake and enjoy immediately!

Notes From Within Recipe

*Apple cider vinegar has a nice "bite" to it but if you don't have any use another sharp tasting vinegar like white balsamic vinegar, white wine vinegar, or rice wine vinegar.

** Ritz crackers are the preferred cracker (better overall buttery and delicious taste) but any cracker will be fine, use saltine style, whole wheat, rice or other crackers that you have.

***Salmon cakes can be made up to one day ahead of time or make and freeze for up to 1 month well wrapped/sealed. Defrost overnight in the refrigerator before sautéing.

Salmon Caesar Salad

Yield: 1 to 2 servings

Crunchy romaine lettuce, creamy Caesar dressing, and roasted salmon make a salad fit for royalty.

For the dressing:
3 tablespoons freshly squeezed lemon juice
1 tablespoon red wine vinegar
1 teaspoon minced garlic
2 teaspoons Worcestershire sauce
2 teaspoons Dijon mustard
10 tablespoons olive oil
Salt and freshly ground pepper
For the salad:
3–4 tablespoons dressing*
3 cups roughly torn romaine lettuce
2 tablespoons freshly grated Parmesan cheese
½ cup croutons (optional)
¼ cup slightly crumbled Classic Roasted Salmon (see recipe page 101)

To make the dressing:

In a medium sized bowl that is set on a moist towel (prevents the bowl from sliding around), whisk together the lemon juice, mustard, red wine vinegar, minced garlic, and Worcestershire sauce. Start to add the olive oil in a very thin stream whisking vigorously. If you start to see an edge of oil around the top, stop adding the olive oil and just whisk for a moment; and then begin again with adding the olive oil. About half way through adding the oil, the dressing will start to thicken. Continue whisking and adding the oil until the dressing is thick enough to coat a spoon with just a few drops falling off the spoon slowly. It may take slightly more or less oil to get the right consistency depending on the kind of mustard and the speed of the whisking involved. Either way it will not be more than a tablespoon or two difference.

Taste for seasoning and add the salt and pepper. The dressing should be fairly tart and bold.

Note: Another method to use for mixing the dressing would be with a hand blender: in a tall container, mix the lemon juice, red wine vinegar, garlic, Worcestershire sauce and Dijon mustard. Add the olive oil in a thin stream with the hand blender running until the dressing is nice and creamy. Season to taste with salt and pepper.

To make the salad:

In a large bowl, lightly mix the lettuce with the cheese, croutons (if using), and about 3 tablespoons of the dressing. Mix well and mound onto a plate. In the same bowl, mix the salmon with the extra dressing still left in the bowl (you just want enough to flavor the salmon without overwhelming it). Top the salad with the salmon and serve.

Notes From Within Recipe

* Any dressing that may be leftover can be used to dress other salads, to toss steamed vegetables in or drizzle a tablespoon or two on rice, potatoes or pasta. The dressing will keep for a week in the refrigerator.

Salmon and Fennel Benedict with Buerre Blanc Sauce

Yield: 1–2 servings

An elegant weekend breakfast or really nice breakfast for dinner!

1 each English muffin or slices of good bread, lightly toasted

1–2 eggs per person (depends on how hungry you are!)

¼ cup Classic Roasted Salmon—see recipe page 101, slightly crumbled and warmed

1 teaspoon white vinegar or fresh lemon juice

3 cups water

Flavor Blast!

1 tablespoon minced fennel (either the top fronds or the bulb; whatever you have)

1 tablespoon minced red onion

1 teaspoon minced Italian parsley

¼ cup dry white wine

1 tablespoon white wine vinegar

½ cup good unsalted butter; at room temperature for at least 10 minutes.

-The butter should be just slightly soft but not very soft or melted (better too chilled than too warm).

For the buerre blanc sauce:

A beurre blanc sauce is a sauce that is a bit easier to make then hollandaise but it is still rich and creamy. The secret is using a great butter! Unsalted is best but if don't have it, you can still make the sauce with salted butter. Just be extra careful in how you season it since there's already some salt in there. This particular beurre blanc recipe is a twist on the classic style.

In a small sauté pan, mix the *Flavor Blast!* ingredients together (the fennel, red onion, minced parsley, white wine, and the white wine vinegar) on low heat until syrupy; about 5–6 minutes.

Remove from the heat and let the pan cool for about 3–4 minutes. Return the pan to VERY LOW heat and begin adding the butter 1 tablespoon at a time, whisking vigorously after each addition, for about 30 seconds. When all the butter has been added, the sauce will have a fluid but creamy/opaque-ish appearance. Taste for seasoning and adjust to your taste. This is a sauce that is used immediately.

To assemble the salmon benedicts:

Set the toasted English muffins or bread on a plate and divide the salmon evenly among the bread. Prepare the poached egg to add on top:

To do so, in a 1-quart saucepan, bring the 3 cups water with the 1 teaspoon of vinegar or lemon juice to a boil. Reduce the heat to a simmer and swirl the water with a spoon then gently crack the egg into the swirling water. The swirl will make the whites fold back on themselves and makes a nice compact poached egg.* Poach the egg about 2½ minutes or to desired doneness. Remove the eggs from the water with a slotted spoon letting any water drip away. Place each egg onto the salmon. Spoon the beurre blanc on top of the poached egg. Sprinkle with any extra fennel you have. This adds a delicious little *Flavor Blast* there at the end. SO yummy!

NOTE: For a delicious gluten-free option, put the benedict in a large lettuce leaf instead of on the English muffin.

Note From Within Recipe

*See our blog, *http://karenandcaroleverybite.wordpress.com*, on how to make the perfect poached egg!

Last Bite Recipe: Salmon Stuffed Pasta Shells with Tomato Sauce & Peas

Yield: 1–2 servings (with potential lunch leftovers; depending on how hungry you are for dinner!)

Comfort food at its finest. A great way to finish up that salmon you made as to do it in a tasty fashion!

8 large pasta shells

2 teaspoons salt

1 cup Ricotta cheese (low or non-fat is fine)

2 tablespoons Parmesan cheese—freshly grated

1 tablespoon minced red onion

½ cup Classic Roasted Salmon (see recipe, page 101), slightly crumbled

2 teaspoons olive oil

Flavor Blast!
1 tablespoon minced fennel
1 teaspoon minced garlic
2 tablespoons minced celery
1 tablespoon minced fresh Italian parsley (optional—okay to leave out if you don't have any on hand)

1 (15-ounce) canned tomatoes in juice

½ cup fresh or frozen peas

Salt and pepper to taste

In a 1-quart saucepan, heat 3 cups of water with the 2 teaspoons of salt added to the pot once it's boiling. When the water is at a strong boil, add the large pasta shells and cook according to package instructions (or about 8–10 minutes), stirring occasionally. Drain well, and rinse with cold water to stop the cooking process. Set aside.

While the pasta is cooking, make the salmon filling:

In a small bowl, mix the ricotta and Parmesan cheese together. Add the minced red onions and mix again. Then add the crumbled salmon, mixing just enough to combine. You don't want to over-mix and make mush!

Stuff 2–3 tablespoons of filling into each cooled pasta shell. Place each shell open side down into a baking dish large enough to hold all the shells without packing then too tightly together.*

For the tomato sauce with peas:**

In a 2-quart saucepan on medium high heat, add the olive oil and heat for 30 seconds. Add the *Flavor Blast!* ingredients (the fennel, garlic, celery and Italian parsley), and cook for about 4–5 minutes; or until the garlic is just starting to brown. Add the tomatoes and juice and reduce the heat to medium, stirring and breaking up the tomatoes with a wooden spoon or fork. Add in the peas. Continue to cook about 15 minutes or until the sauce is a little chunky but looking like a nice sauce***.

When the sauce is done, spoon over the stuffed pasta shells and bake at 375°F for about 30 minutes, or until hot and bubbly.

Notes From Within Recipe

* Pasta shells can be made up to this point a day ahead or you can make and freeze right away for later eating.

**While peas are a nice vegetable addition (and a great way to use up some extra frozen peas you might have in your freezer), it is not essential to the sauce. It's okay to leave them out if you don't have them!

***We know that sounds arbitrary but it will look like a great sauce when it's done. We like a little bit of the tomato pieces still evident in the sauce, and not so pureed that it looks just like a can of tomato sauce!

Recipe Notes

_____

_____

_____

_____

_____

_____

_____

_____

_____

_____

_____

_____

_____

_____

_____

_____

Chapter 6

Everyday Seafood

Seafood leftovers don't heat up well, and the fish can start to smell (and annoy your coworkers if you take it in for lunch), so the recipes in this chapter provide smaller portions instead, with some carry through to later recipes, but not as frequently as other chapters.

Quinoa with Yogurt, Cucumbers, and Sautéed Shrimp

Yield: 2 servings

Quinoa is one of the world's most ancient grains and is very healthy. The contrast of spicy shrimp and cooling yogurt sauce makes for a delicious meal anytime. We really kick it up in this recipe and have not one but TWO *Flavor Blasts*!

For the quinoa:
½ cup quinoa
1 teaspoon vegetable soup base (optional)*
1 cup chicken stock, vegetable stock, or water

For the yogurt sauce:
1/3 cup plain or lemon-flavored yogurt (low-fat or nonfat is fine)
1 tablespoon minced red onion
1 teaspoon minced garlic
1 medium English cucumber, finely diced (about 1 cup)**
½ teaspoon salt
¼ teaspoon freshly ground black pepper

For the shrimp:
2 tablespoons olive oil
8–10 large shrimp***

1st *Flavor Blast!*****
2 teaspoons sweet paprika
4 teaspoons minced fresh Italian parsley
1 teaspoon ground cumin
¾ teaspoon salt
1 teaspoon freshly ground black pepper

2nd *Flavor Blast!*
½ teaspoon lemon zest
½ teaspoon minced garlic
½ teaspoon minced fresh Italian parsley
½ teaspoon sweet paprika

To make the quinoa and yogurt sauce:

In a small saucepan with a tight-fitting lid, mix the quinoa with the vegetable base, if using, and stock or water, and bring the liquid to a boil. Reduce the heat to low and cover the pan. Cook the quinoa for about 20 minutes. You can tell it's done when it has absorbed all of the liquid, looks fluffy, and has an overall lighter color. Stir, cover again, and let rest for 5 minutes before using.

While the quinoa cooks, make the yogurt sauce. In a small bowl, mix all the ingredients together. Let the sauce sit for at least 10 minutes so the flavors have a chance to blend.

To make the shrimp:

Heat a medium skillet over medium-high heat for 1 minute, then add the olive oil and wait for 30 seconds. Add the shrimp to the hot pan. As soon as they start to turn pink on one side (about 3 to 4 minutes), flip them over and add the 1st *Flavor Blast!* ingredients (the paprika, Italian parsley, cumin, salt, and pepper). Once they turn pink on the other side (at most, only another couple of minutes), take the pan off the heat.

To assemble the dish:

Mix the 2nd *Flavor Blast!* ingredients (the lemon zest, garlic, Italian parsley, and sweet paprika) together in a small bowl. Mound the quinoa on a plate and make a crater in the center. Place the shrimp in the crater, spoon the yogurt sauce on top, and sprinkle with the 2nd *Flavor Blast!* mixture.

Notes From Within Recipe

*Vegetable base is a rich, thick paste made with sautéed onions, celery, and carrots. The concentrated flavor, while not essential, helps kick up this dish overall.

You can easily make your own vegetable base with leftover trimmings from carrots, onions, onion peels, garlic, garlic peels, mushroom stem ends, celery ends, and bits of herbs.

Put everything in a pot with cold water and simmer about 30 minutes. Drain into a bowl with a sieve to catch the trimmings and your vegetable base is ready to use. It can also be frozen or will keep up to 4 days in the refrigerator.

**If you don't have an English cucumber, a regular cucumber will work fine as well.

***Most grocery stores now sell shrimp that has already been peeled and deveined (fresh or frozen). If you buy whole shrimp, you'll want to clean, peel, and devein them. Rinse them off thoroughly with cold water, and peel the shell off. Along the backside of the shrimp is a long, thin black tubule. This is actually the digestive tract of the shrimp and definitely needs to be removed. Then either keep the tails on, or pull them off and you're ready to go. To see a detailed video on how to clean, peel and devein shrimp, visit our blog: (*http://karenandcaroleverybite.wordpress.com*).
So while you certainly can get fresh shrimp and clean them up as described, we think it's easier just to go ahead and get them peeled and deveined!

Remember to save those shells in the freezer until you have enough to make a great shrimp stock for soups, sauces, chowders or other recipes.

****Shrimp takes very little time to cook, so have your *Flavor Blast!* ingredients measured and ready to go. You don't want to overcook the shrimp while you're searching through your spice cabinet, as they will turn rubbery and become not very tasty.

Perfect Clams with Linguini

Yield: 2 servings

A great weeknight meal: fast, easy, and oh-so-tasty! Garlic bread makes a nice side dish for "sopping" up the yummy sauce (see chapter 3).

2 quarts water
1 tablespoon salt
2 ounces dried linguini (about a quarter-size portion)*
2 tablespoons olive oil

Flavor Blast!
2 cloves garlic, smashed flat as a piece of paper
2 tablespoons minced fresh Italian parsley
½ to 1 teaspoon red pepper flakes (depending on how much heat you want!)

½ cup dry white wine
1 cup greens, roughly chopped (kale, arugula, or escarole)
1 lb. littleneck or other local clams, scrubbed well on the outside to remove sand and grit

In a large saucepan, bring the water and salt to a vigorous boil. Add the linguini and stir well. Cook according to package instructions, about 8 to 9 minutes, stirring often.

While the pasta cooks, heat a large skillet over medium-high heat for 1 minute. Add the olive oil and wait for 30 seconds. Add the garlic and parsley part of the *Flavor Blast!* ingredients — the parsley will sputter and make a frying sound, which is just what you want.

Cook for about 30 to 45 seconds, and then add the red pepper flakes (the last of the *Flavor Blast!*, if desired), clams, and wine. Cover the skillet with a tight fitting lid. Gently shake the pan a few times to move everything around, and cook for about 4 to 5 minutes, or until the clams open. Remove the lid, reduce the heat to low, and discard any unopened clams.*** Add the greens and gently stir.

The linguini should be done at about the same time as the clams. Drain it and add it to the clams, tossing the pasta for at least 2 or 3 minutes to allow it to absorb some of the cooking liquid. The starch from the pasta will also thicken the sauce. Serve in a deep bowl with an empty bowl alongside for the clam shells.

Notes From Within Recipe

*The term "quarter-size portion" means that when you hold the pasta with your thumb and index finger wrapped around it, what's inside is about the size of a quarter.

**To properly store uncooked clams, put them in a bowl, and put a damp kitchen towel down over them in the bowl. DO NOT submerge them fully in cold water or put them on ice, or cover with plastic wrap. The water will actually shock and kill them because of a lack of oxygen. You just want to keep them cool. Use the clams within 2 days MAX (24 hours is best). Discard any with shells that stay open (or any that don't close when tapped, or are broken—better yet don't buy those!)

***If clams have not opened up after 4 to 5 minutes of cooking, they either were dead before you cooked them or were filled with sand and mud. These are not good for eating. Discard immediately.

Mediterranean Mussels with Vermouth and Orzo

Yield: 1 to 2 servings

Mussels love dry vermouth like tomatoes love basil, making this a simple yet satisfying dish. Be sure to serve it with a toasted baguette to "sop" up all the liquid yumminess. Mediterranean mussels are a type of mussel available in the Pacific Northwest.

If you can't find Mediterranean mussels, just use any other local mussel. When buying mussels, make sure that any open shells close quickly when touched or shaken and that none of the shells are already broken. Mussels should feel a little heavy in comparison to their size — you want mussel meat, not shell!

3 cups water

1 tablespoon salt

½ cup orzo (rice-shaped pasta)

1 tablespoon olive oil

1 clove garlic, smashed flat as a piece of paper

2 tablespoons minced fresh Italian parsley

4 ounces cremini mushrooms (about 4), thinly sliced*

1 lb. Mediterranean mussels, debearded and scrubbed free from sand and grit**

1 cup fresh tomatoes, roughly chopped***

½ teaspoon red pepper flakes (optional)

2 tablespoons dry vermouth or other dry white wine (or water)

In a small saucepan, boil the water and add the salt and orzo. Stir and cook according to package instructions, about 8 to 10 minutes. Drain and set aside.

Heat a medium saucepan with a tight-fitting lid over medium-high heat for 1 minute, add the olive oil, and wait for 30 seconds. Add the garlic, parsley, and mushrooms and sauté for about 3 to 4 minutes, or until the mushrooms have taken on a deep, rich brown color and have released their juices. Add the mussels, tomatoes, red pepper flakes, and vermouth (or white wine). Reduce the heat to medium and cover the pan. Cook for about 3 to 5 minutes, or until the mussels have opened. Discard any unopened mussels. Taste the sauce and season with salt and pepper if necessary.

Add the orzo to the mussel sauce and cook for another moment or two to allow the flavors to mingle. Serve in a deep bowl with an empty bowl alongside for the mussel shells.

Notes From Within Recipe

*Remember: small brown=more flavor! Rinse them quickly to remove any dirt or grit and pat them dry with a napkin or paper towel before slicing.

**Most mussels have what is commonly called a "beard." The beard is made of fibers called byssal threads that emerge from the mussel's shell near the bottom (or the "hinge") and are what they use to hold onto rocks in the water. It's best to buy mussels with the beards still attached because removing them causes the mussel to die. Dead mussels are not to be eaten because they break down very quickly and can cause severe food poisoning.

To debeard a mussel, hold it in one hand, cover the other hand with a dry towel, and grasp the beard; give it a sharp yank toward the hinge and then discard. See our video (*http://karenandcaroleverybite.wordpress.com*) for a lesson on how to debeard a mussel.

To properly store uncooked mussels, put them in a bowl, and put a damp kitchen towel down over them in the bowl. DO NOT submerge them fully in cold water or and then cover with plastic wrap. The water will actually shock and kill them because of a lack of oxygen. You just want to keep them cool. Use the mussels within 2 days <u>MAX</u> (24 hours is best). Discard any with shells that stay open (or any that don't close when tapped).

*** you can also use canned tomatoes, and freeze the leftovers for another recipe.

Spicy Mexican Baked Cod

Yield: 1 to 2 servings

This is one of Carol's favorites and has been made in her family for years. An oldie but a goodie!

2 (5-ounce each) cod fillets
1/3 cup salsa

Flavor Blast!
½ teaspoon chili powder
Pinch of cayenne pepper (optional)

1/3 cup shredded sharp Cheddar cheese
2 tablespoons plus 2 teaspoons coarsely crushed corn chips (just a small bag from the vending machine will be sufficient!)
1 small avocado, peeled, pitted, and sliced
2 tablespoons sour cream
1 tablespoon chopped fresh cilantro

Preheat oven to 400°F. Lightly grease a small baking dish.

Rinse the cod fillets under cold water, and pat dry with paper towels. Place them side by side in the prepared baking dish. In a small bowl, mix the salsa with the *Flavor Blast!* ingredients (the chili powder and cayenne pepper, if using) and pour the salsa mixture over the top of the fish. Sprinkle evenly with the shredded cheese, and top with the crushed corn chips.

Bake, uncovered, in the preheated oven for 15 minutes, or until fish is opaque and flakes with a fork. Serve topped with sliced avocado and sour cream. Sprinkle with chopped cilantro if desired.

Tilapia with Garlic-Roasted Tomatoes

Yield: 1 to 2 servings

Tilapia is a great-tasting and inexpensive fish that is perfect for pairing with roasted tomatoes. Serving with Heavenly Herbed Rice (see recipe page 155) for an easy side dish.

2 Roma tomatoes, cut in half lengthwise and cored
1 tablespoon plus 2 teaspoons olive oil, divided
2 teaspoons minced garlic
1 tablespoon minced fresh basil leaves, or 1 teaspoon dried
Salt and freshly ground black pepper
2 (5-ounce each) tilapia fillets
½ recipe Heavenly Herbed Rice (see recipe, page 155)—optional

Preheat the oven to 400°F.

In a medium bowl, toss the tomatoes with 1 tablespoon of the olive oil, garlic, basil, and a pinch of salt and pepper. Lay the tomatoes out on a small baking sheet and bake for about 20 minutes. Remove the sheet from the oven and set aside. Keep the oven at 400°F.

Place the fillets in a small baking dish side by side without touching. Drizzle the remaining 2 teaspoons of oil over them and season with a pinch of salt and pepper. Spoon the roasted tomatoes around the edges of the fillets and spoon any roasting liquid onto the fillets. Bake the fish for about 8 to 10 minutes, depending on how thick the fillets are. Thinner fillets will take less time, and thicker fillets may take a moment or two longer. The fish is done when it gives slightly when pressed with a fork.

Serve the fish on a plate with the rice on the side, if desired.

Last Bite Recipe: Rustic Rice and Seafood Cakes with Spicy Sauce

Yield: 1 to 2 servings

We love these little crispy cakes! You can either use a variety of seafood you've picked up from the store, or anything left from a previous recipe in this chapter. Use up those last bites of seafood if you can!

For the seafood cakes:

1 cup Heavenly Herbed Rice (page 155)

1 egg, lightly whisked

2 teaspoons cornstarch

1 tablespoon olive oil

½ cup Panko breadcrumbs

9 pieces of either shrimp, clams, or mussels* (any option or combination thereof... use up what you might have leftover from a previous recipe, or grab a few more at the seafood market).

2 cloves garlic, smashed flat as a piece of paper

1 tablespoon minced fresh Italian parsley

For the sauce:

2 tablespoons olive oil

2 tablespoons fresh tomatoes, finely diced**

Flavor Blast!

1 tablespoon capers, drained and minced

1 teaspoon red pepper flakes

1 tablespoon freshly squeezed lemon juice

2 tablespoons minced onion

½ teaspoon garlic

1 teaspoon finely chopped Italian parsley

Salt and freshly ground pepper

2 tablespoons vegetable or canola oil

To make the cakes:

In a medium bowl, mix the rice, egg, and cornstarch. Set aside.

Heat a medium sauté pan with a tight-fitting lid over medium-high heat for about a minute. Add the olive oil, wait for 30 seconds, and then add your uncooked shellfish (the shrimp, clams, or mussels), garlic, and parsley, and sauté for 1 minute. Cover and cook for about 3 to 4 minutes (or until the shellfish have opened if using clams or mussels). Remove the pan from the heat, remove the shellfish from the pan (removing the clams and mussels from their shells if needed), and finely chop.*** Mix the seafood together with the rice, egg, and cornstarch mixture. Form into cakes about 3 inches wide by ½ inch thick (Note: the mixture will be somewhat sticky). Coat the cakes in the panko, making sure to cover them completely and pressing the crumbs to help them adhere.**** Set aside.

To make the sauce:

In a small bowl, mix the olive oil, diced tomatoes and all of the *Flavor Blast!* ingredients together. Taste and add salt and pepper if needed.

To prepare the dish:

Heat a small sauté pan over medium-high heat for 1 minute, add the vegetable or canola oil, and heat for 30 seconds. When the oil is hot, add the seafood cakes and fry them until they're golden brown, about 3 minutes, then flip them and brown them on the other side. Serve them on a plate topped with the spicy sauce. Sprinkle with additional salt and pepper if desired.

Notes From Within Recipe

*How to debeard a mussel: *http://karenandcaroleverybite.wordpress.com.*
**You can also use any canned tomatoes you have frozen from a previous recipe.
***Finely smash the discarded shells, and you can use them as garden fertilizer!
****Moisten your hands with a little water before forming the cakes. This will help the cakes not stick to your fingers while forming.

Recipe Notes

_____

_____

_____

_____

_____

_____

_____

_____

_____

_____

_____

_____

_____

_____

_____

_____

Chapter 7

Meatless Mondays and Beyond

Victory Garden Polenta with Tomato Sauce and Greens

Yield: 2 servings

Victory Gardens were gardens planted at both private and public locations during World Wars I & II to reduce the pressure on the public food supply brought on by the war effort. These gardens were considered "morale boosters" because the gardeners really felt they had made an important contribution to themselves and others, and because of that, they became part of daily life.

1 ½ cups chicken or vegetable stock (or water)

1/8 teaspoon salt

¼ teaspoon freshly ground black pepper

1/8 teaspoon cayenne pepper

1/3 cup polenta

½ tablespoon olive oil

¼ cup finely diced onions

¼ cup finely diced cremini or other fresh mushroom

1 tablespoon minced garlic

1 tablespoon minced fresh Italian parsley

¼ cup corn kernels, fresh or frozen and thawed

1 tablespoon shredded fresh basil leaves

1 recipe Zippy Tomato Sauce (page 196), or other good canned variety

4 cups kale, collards, or spinach torn or roughly cut into small pieces

In a small saucepan, bring the stock to a boil. Add the salt, pepper, and cayenne, and reduce the heat to medium. Add the polenta in a thin, steady stream while stirring constantly with a spoon.* Stir frequently until the polenta starts to thicken, about 5 to 6 minutes. Reduce the heat to medium-low and continue to cook (while periodically stirring) until the polenta starts to pull away from the side of the saucepan, about 20 to 25 minutes. The polenta grains will be soft but not mushy.

While the polenta is cooking, in a medium sauté pan, heat the olive oil over medium-high heat until it's hot but not smoking. Add the onions, and sauté for 2 to 3 minutes, or until they're just starting to become transparent. Add the mushrooms and garlic and continue to sauté until they're lightly browned, about 3 to 4 minutes more. Stir in the parsley and corn, and set aside. Once the polenta has finished cooking, add the vegetables to it and mix well. Add in the basil and set aside.**

In a medium saucepan over medium heat, simmer the tomato sauce for 5 minutes to warm it up thoroughly, and then add the kale or collards, and reduce the heat to low. Cook for about 8 to 10 minutes, until the greens are soft but not mushy. (If you're using spinach, cook it for only 3 to 4 minutes, or until it's just wilted).***

To serve, cut pieces of the polenta out (the polenta will set up once cooled) and serve on top of the wilted greens. Top with sauce.

Notes From Within Recipe

*If you add the polenta all at once, it has a tendency to lump; once you have lumps in your polenta, you'll never get them out. And nobody likes lumpy polenta!

**Another option instead of simply spooning the polenta onto your plate when ready is to pour the polenta into a greased 9x13-inch jelly roll pan (or any size pan) and spread the polenta out evenly. While you're finishing with the rest of the recipe, the polenta will set up and you can easily cut out a variety of shapes and designs. It just jazzes up the appearance of the polenta a bit and would be something you might consider if having company for dinner, etc.

And if you have the time, you can also take the pieces and brown them up in a skillet that's been warming with about 2 tablespoons of oil in it for a few minutes. Just gives it a nice crust on it, but is definitely not critical to the dish. That is what we did in the recipe photo above.

***Hearty greens like kale and collards need to be cooked a bit more than softer greens like spinach to break down the fibers for easier digestion.

We've often kept the sauce and greens separate when cooking (as in the recipe photo), but certainly combining as the recipe calls for is delicious as well. There are many varieties to this dish, and that is one reason we love it so!

Easy Thai Curry with Vegetables and Rice

Yield: 2 servings

Enjoy this easy, weeknight Thai meal without having to go out to a restaurant! The secret is to cook the vegetables for different amounts of time, depending on their tenderness: for example, veggies such as carrots and winter squash are harder and will take longer to cook, while celery, peppers, zucchini, mushrooms, asparagus, green beans, etcetera are softer and will take less time.

½ tablespoon vegetable oil

1½ tablespoons red curry paste*

1 teaspoon minced garlic

1 teaspoon fresh ginger, peeled and grated

3 cups seasonal vegetables chopped into ½-inch pieces and kept separate to add to recipe at different times

1 (15-ounce) can coconut milk

Zest from ½ lime**

¼ cup fresh Thai basil leaves***

2 cups cooked rice (any kind you prefer)

2 tablespoons roughly chopped fresh cilantro leaves, for garnish (optional)****

Heat a large saucepan over medium heat. When the pan is hot, add the vegetable oil and wait for 30 seconds.

When the oil is hot, add the curry paste, garlic, ginger, and onions, if using. Sauté until the spices are fragrant and the onions are translucent, about 5 minutes.

Add the coconut milk and any of the vegetables that will need to cook a bit longer (such as parsnips, onions, celery, carrots, potatoes), and simmer until they're halfway cooked, about 10 to 15 minutes.

Then add the more tender vegetables (such as peppers, asparagus, or mushrooms) and continue to cook until they're almost done (not quite fully tender); about 8 additional minutes. Add the lime zest and basil and continue to simmer for another 5 minutes.

Serve over rice, and garnished with cilantro if desired.

Notes From Within Recipe

*Thai curry paste is available in most major grocery stores and comes in the following varieties:

> Green: Great with meat and seafood, especially mussels and noodles
> Yellow: For chicken and other poultry, soups, and noodles
> Red: Fairly spicy and great for meats, vegetables, and noodles
> Panang: Similar to red curry paste and influenced by Malaysian flavors; for tofu, beans, and curries with little or no vegetables

**You can sprinkle some of the lime juice from the zested lime over your meal, once it's assembled. If you don't use it, you can always compost it!
***Thai basil needs to be cooked to fully bring out its amazing flavor.
***Any extra basil you have can be placed in a sealable bag and stored in the refrigerator (if using soon) for 3–5 days or frozen for up to a month.
****Definitely use any frozen you might have saved from a previous recipe.

Potato Pie with Vegetables, Whipped Tofu, and Gruyère

Yield: 1 to 2 servings*

This is an easy, layered dish with a delicious blend of flavors and textures. Serve it with a salad and crusty bread.

3 cups water

2 teaspoons salt

½ pound Yukon gold potatoes, cut into ¼-inch-thick slices

1 tablespoon olive oil

¼ cup finely diced onions

½ cup finely diced zucchini

1 clove garlic, smashed flat as a piece of paper

Flavor Blast!

2 tablespoons minced fresh Italian parsley

2 teaspoons minced fresh thyme, or ½ teaspoon dried

¼ cup diced tomatoes in juice*

½ teaspoon freshly ground black pepper

1 tablespoon shredded fresh basil leaves (or use what you have on hand; frozen from a previous recipe)

½ pound soft tofu, drained**

Salt and freshly ground black pepper

¼ cup shredded Gruyère cheese

In a large saucepan, heat the 3 cups of water to boiling. When the water is boiling, add 2 teaspoons of the salt and the potatoes. Reduce the heat to medium and cook the potatoes until they're just tender, about 12 minutes. Drain them and spread them out in a small baking dish.*** Set aside.

Heat a medium sauté pan over medium-high heat for 1 minute, add the olive oil and wait for 30 seconds. When the oil is hot, add the onions, zucchini, and garlic. Sauté for about 5 to 6 minutes, or until the onions are translucent and the garlic and zucchini are just starting to brown. Add the *Flavor Blast!* ingredients (the Italian parsley, thyme, tomatoes and black pepper) and sauté for 3 to 4 minutes more. Add the basil and mix well. Taste the mixture and add salt and pepper if needed, then spoon it over the potatoes, making sure the vegetables get in all the nooks and crannies.

Preheat the oven to 375°F.

Place the tofu in a bowl. Using a hand blender, hand mixer, or whisk, whip the tofu until it's nice and creamy. Season it with a pinch of salt and pepper. Spoon the tofu over the vegetables and sprinkle the Gruyère on top.

Bake the pie for about 30 minutes, or until the tofu has set. You'll know it's set if it jiggles like Jell-o when you gently shake it. The pie will be slightly puffy as well. Let it rest for 5 to 7 minutes before cutting and eating.

Notes From Within Recipe

*Again, you can use either fresh or canned tomatoes. If you're using canned tomatoes, freeze the unused portion and use it for another meal, such as Chicken Tortilla Soup (page 38), Pork Tacos with Roasted Chilies (page 78), Meatloaf Hash with Poached Egg (page 95), or Two-Alarm Braised Greens and Rice (page 148).

**To drain tofu, simply place it between several layers of paper towels and allow it to sit for about 15 minutes. This process removes excess moisture, allowing more flavor to be absorbed while cooking.

A great use of that extra ½ pound of tofu (if you get it in the 1lb package at the store) is to make a chocolate tofu pie with it! Simply mix 8 ounces of melted chocolate with the 8 ounces of tofu (slightly whipped first before adding it together with the chocolate), until smooth. Pour into a prebaked pie shell and pop it in the refrigerator until set and smooth (at least 2 hours). And voila! A yummy, healthy, and best of all, easy pie!

***You can also make individual servings (as in picture at the beginning of the recipe).

Baby Kale Salad with White Beans and Mustard Vinaigrette

Yield: 1 to 2 servings

This is a salad that definitely eats more like a meal. Enjoy it for lunch or dinner with crusty bread.

3 cups baby kale*

2 very thin slices red onion

½ of a stalk of very thinly sliced celery

(slice at a slight angle for a pretty presentation)

1 Roma tomato, halved lengthwise and thinly sliced

½ (15-ounce) can white beans (cannellini, navy, or other small white bean), rinsed and drained

¼ cup Mustard Vinaigrette (recipe follows)

In a large bowl, mix the kale with the onions, celery, tomatoes, and beans. Add the vinaigrette and toss well.

Note From Within Recipe

*Baby kale is not as tough as full-grown kale, so it doesn't need to be cooked. It's becoming more available in grocery stores and can also be purchased at farmers' markets. If you can't find it, use any greens you already have or can easily find. We personally love escarole, beet greens, arugula, or butter lettuce.

Mustard Vinaigrette

Yield: 1 cup

This vinaigrette will keep, tightly covered, in the refrigerator for up to a week. It can be used in other salads, or as even a simple dressing to freshly sliced tomatoes. Yum!

2 tablespoons Dijon mustard
1 tablespoon minced shallot
2 teaspoons dried basil
1/3 cup white balsamic vinegar*
½ cup olive oil
Salt and freshly ground black pepper

In a deep bowl, mix the mustard, shallot, basil, and vinegar. Using a hand blender or whisk, mix for 30 seconds. Place a moist towel on the table and place the bowl on top (this will stop the bowl from spinning as you whisk). Begin adding the olive oil in a thin stream while running the blender or whisking vigorously. The vinaigrette will be a little thick and pretty tart. Season to taste with salt and pepper, and let it sit for a few minutes before using to let the flavors meld.

Note From Within Recipe

*White balsamic vinegar is available in most major supermarkets. It's similar to traditional balsamic vinegar, but a little less sweet and syrupy with a bit of a cleaner aftertaste. It also prevents discoloration of food, so it's sometimes preferred for dressings. If you can't find it, use white wine vinegar or champagne vinegar with a pinch of sugar.

Two-Alarm Braised Greens and Rice

Yield: 1 to 2 servings

Spicy greens on a bed of rice is so satisfying. The two alarms are jalapeño and cayenne pepper. They really give the greens a nice burst of flavor, but aren't critical for a delicious dish, so leave them out if you prefer no alarms!

1 cup water
½ cup long-grain rice (such as jasmine or basmati)
1 tablespoon olive oil
¼ cup finely diced onions
2 tablespoons minced garlic

Flavor Blast!
1 tablespoon minced fresh Italian parsley
½ jalapeño, minced (remove seeds and membranes for less heat)
Pinch of cayenne pepper (optional)
3 cups roughly chopped greens, such as kale, collards, mustard greens, escarole,
Swiss chard, beet or radish greens
½ cup diced tomatoes*
1 teaspoon salt
1 teaspoon freshly ground black pepper

In a small saucepan, boil the water, add in the rice, and stir. Reduce the heat to medium-low and cover the pan with a tight-fitting lid. Cook for about 20 minutes, or until all the water has been absorbed and the rice is tender. Remove the pan from the heat, fluff the rice with a fork, cover again, and let rest for 5 minutes before serving.

While the rice cooks, heat a medium saucepan over medium-high heat for 1 minute. Add the olive oil, wait for 30 seconds, and add in the onions and garlic; stirring well. Cook for about 4 to 5 minutes, or until the onions are translucent and the garlic is just starting to brown. Add the *Flavor Blast!* ingredients (the Italian parsley, jalapeno, and cayenne pepper) and sauté for an additional minute. Be careful not to inhale the jalapeno fumes when they're first cooking; they can be rather strong! Reduce the heat to medium and add the greens, tomatoes, salt and pepper. Mix well, cover with a tight-fitting lid, and cook for about 10 minutes.

Remove the lid and stir. Continue cooking until the greens are wilted and tender, about 15 to 20 minutes total.

Ladle the greens over the rice and serve.

Note From Within Recipe

*either fresh, canned, or frozen and thawed tomatoes can be used.

Whole Grain Tortilla with Tofu Scramble

Yield: 1 to 2 servings

This is a great way to start your day, and you only need to add about 15 minutes to your morning. It's totally worth it — these tortillas are loaded with nutrition and flavor. Or make several and freeze them for a quick breakfast or late-night snack. Just pop them in a microwave or warm them in a dry skillet over low heat for about 4 minutes per side, or until hot.

4 ounces firm tofu—patted dry and diced into ¼-inch cubes
2 teaspoons olive oil
2 tablespoons finely diced onions
2 teaspoons minced garlic

Flavor Blast!
1 teaspoon ground cumin
½ teaspoon sweet paprika
¼ teaspoon dried oregano
¼ teaspoon salt
1/8 teaspoon freshly ground black pepper

1 to 3 teaspoons minced jalapeño, depending on how much heat you want
2 tablespoons finely diced tomatoes*
¼ (15-ounce) can black beans, drained and rinsed**
1 to 2 (8-inch) whole-grain or corn tortillas

Heat a medium nonstick skillet over medium-high heat for 1 minute, add the olive oil, and wait for 30 seconds. When the oil is hot, add the tofu cubes. Sauté for 3 to 4 minutes, or until the tofu is starting to brown and get crispy on all sides. Remove the tofu to a plate and set aside.

In the same skillet, add the onions and garlic and sauté for 2 minutes. Add the *Flavor Blast!* ingredients (the cumin, paprika, oregano, salt, and pepper) and sauté for 30 seconds.*** Add the jalapeños, tomatoes, tofu, and black beans and sauté until hot, about 3 minutes.

Heat a separate skillet over medium-high heat for 1 minute. Lay the tortilla(s) in the skillet and heat for about 2 minutes per side, or until the tortilla is flexible and slightly toasted. Remove the tortilla(s) to a plate. Mound the vegetable and tofu mixture into the tortilla(s), fold the side edges in, and then roll up the tortilla like a cigar. Serve immediately.

Notes From Within Recipe

*Either fresh, canned, or frozen and thawed tomatoes can be used.

**Extra beans can be used in a salad or frozen for later use.

***When you sauté dry spices and herbs, it allows their volatile oils to be released into food, adding a lot more flavor.

Revitalizing Rice and Vegetable Stew

Yield: 1 to 2 servings

A meal that will lift your spirits and body.

1 cup water
½ cup jasmine rice

Flavor Blast!
1 teaspoon fresh ginger, grated and peeled*
½ teaspoon lemon zest
½ teaspoon minced fresh Italian parsley
1 tablespoon minced green onions (about one green onion)

1 tablespoon olive oil
2 tablespoons finely diced onions
2 tablespoons diced carrots
2 tablespoons diced celery
1 clove garlic, smashed flat as a piece of paper
½ cup diced winter squash, such as butternut or acorn
1 teaspoon curry powder**
Salt and freshly ground black pepper
1 cup roughly chopped greens, such as kale, collards, mustard greens, escarole, Swiss chard, or beet or radish greens
1 tablespoon minced fresh Italian parsley
1½ cups vegetable or chicken stock

In a small saucepan with a tight-fitting lid, boil the water, add the rice, and stir. Reduce the heat to medium-low and cover the pan. Cook for about 20 minutes, or until all the water has been absorbed and the rice is tender. Remove the pan from the heat, fluff the rice with a fork, cover again, and let rest for 5 minutes before serving.

While the rice cooks, in a small bowl, mix the *Flavor Blast!* ingredients together (the ginger, lemon zest, Italian parsley, and green onions). Set aside.

Heat a medium saucepan with a tight-fitting lid over medium-high heat for 1 minute, add the olive oil, and wait for 30 seconds. When the oil is hot, add the onions, carrots, celery, and garlic and sauté for about 5 to 6 minutes, or until the onions are translucent and the garlic has just started to brown. Add the squash, curry powder, and a pinch of salt and pepper. Sauté for about 1 minute to release the volatile oils in the curry powder. Add the greens and parsley.

Sauté for 2 minutes, or until the greens are slightly wilted, and then add in the stock. Reduce the heat to medium-low, cover, and cook for about 10 minutes.

Remove the lid, reduce the heat to low, and cook until the squash is fork-tender. Ladle the stew over the rice, sprinkle the *Flavor Blast!* ingredients on top, and serve.

Notes From Within Recipe

*When buying fresh ginger at the store, just break off a piece about the size that you'll need. If you do have extra, it can be frozen for up to 2 months.

**Bulk sections of grocery stores are great and are an affordable way to get things like small amounts of spices! So try that first before you have to go somewhere else.

Heavenly Herbed Rice

Yield: 1 to 2 servings

Rice is an endlessly diverse grain. It takes on the flavors you add to the cooking liquid and can accompany almost any meal. Another double *Flavor Blast!* meal!

Pair with Pleasing Pinto Beans (see photo of the two on page 155) for a tasty and satisfying meal.

½ cup jasmine rice
2 teaspoons olive oil

1st Flavor Blast!
2 teaspoons minced garlic
2 teaspoons dry herbs, such as basil, thyme, oregano, marjoram, sage, or any combination
1 teaspoon salt
½ teaspoon freshly ground black pepper

1 cup water

2nd Flavor Blast!
2 tablespoons minced green onion (both white and green parts)
1 tablespoon minced fresh Italian parsley
1 teaspoon lemon zest

In a small saucepan with a tight-fitting lid, mix the rice with the olive oil and the first *Flavor Blast!* ingredients (the garlic, herbs, salt, and pepper). Add the water, cover, and cook the rice over medium-low for 20 minutes. If the pan starts to boil over, reduce the heat to low. <u>Don't</u> stir or disturb the rice in any way, and *don't* remove the lid.*

After 20 minutes, fluff the rice with a fork and let it rest for 5 minutes. Mix in the second *Flavor Blast!* ingredients (the green onion, Italian parsley, and lemon zest) and serve.

Note From Within Recipe

*The reason you cover the rice while it's cooking is so steam doesn't escape, because the steam is what's evenly cooking the rice. By not disturbing it, you get beautiful, fluffy rice.

Pleasing Pinto Beans

Yield: 1 to 2 servings

Full of fiber and flavor, pinto beans are a great way to round out a meal or bulk up soup. Serve them with Heavenly Herbed Rice (as in photo below; see page 155 for that recipe), your favorite salsa, and a sprinkling of chopped cilantro to make a complete protein — and a wonderful vegetarian meal. Or use them in Pork Tacos with Roasted Chilies (page 78) or Tasty Tacos with Tomato Salsa and Cilantro Pesto (page 92).

Note: the beans need to soak for at least eight hours, so allow time accordingly. You could use canned beans as a substitute for cooking your own but often canned beans just aren't nearly as good as making the recipe using fresh cooked beans. This recipe will work for any dried beans. Any cooked beans not used right away can be added to salads, soups or mashed and spread on crostini.

¾ cup dry pinto beans

3 cups water

2 teaspoons salt

2 teaspoons olive oil

3 tablespoons finely diced onions

2 tablespoon finely diced celery*

1 tablespoon minced garlic

1 teaspoon ground cumin

1 tablespoon tomato paste**

¾ cup finely diced fresh tomatoes

Freshly ground black pepper

1½ cup vegetable or chicken stock or water

In a medium bowl, add the beans, water, and salt.*** Soak the beans for at least 8 hours or overnight at room temperature.

Drain the beans. Fill a small saucepan with 3 more cups of fresh water and add the beans. Bring the water to a boil, then reduce the heat, cover with a tight fitting lid, and let the beans simmer until they're tender, about 1 hour.

Heat a medium skillet over medium-high heat for 1 minute, add the olive oil, and wait for 30 seconds. When the oil is hot, add the onions and celery and sauté for about 2 to 3 minutes, or until the onions start to turn translucent. Add the garlic, sauté for 1 minute, add the cumin, and cook for an additional 30 seconds. Add the tomatoes and beans, and season to taste with salt and pepper. Stir well, and add the stock. Bring the beans to a simmer over medium-high heat. Reduce the heat to low and cook for about 15 minutes. Don't boil the beans: just let them simmer and take on the flavors of the other ingredients. Serve immediately or freeze for later use. Cooked beans will keep in the freezer for about 1 month in a well-sealed container.

Notes From Within Recipe

*Here are a few suggestions for what to do with leftover celery:
Chop it into ½-inch pieces and sauté them in a little butter. Sprinkle with toasted sesame seeds for a yummy side dish.

Freeze stalks to use in a soup base (freezing and thawing them will make them kind of limp and soft, but if you're using them in a soup, they'll cook down anyway, and their addition will still flavor the soup immensely.)

Freeze the ends for use in stock.

Fill stalks with goat cheese, peanut butter, or hummus for a great snack.

Another idea on how to use up extra celery is to make the "Braised Celery" recipe referenced in the "Notes From Within Recipe" section on page 82.

**Freeze remaining tomato paste in small amounts for later use (will keep for several months in the freezer).

***When salt is added to the soaking water, a chemical reaction occurs that makes the beans' skin more porous, which helps them cook more quickly later on. Be sure to add the salt in the recipe at the point of soaking; NOT at the point of cooking.

Balsamic-Glazed Carrots

Yield: 1 to 2 servings

Few things are better than roasted carrots tossed in a balsamic vinegar glaze. Simply divine! These make a fantastic addition to almost anything, including Perfect Roasted Chicken (page 27) or the Herb Roasted Turkey Breast with Tomatoes and Cauliflower (page 45).

2 to 3 organic carrots, sliced ¼ inch thick on an angle (about 2 cups)
1 tablespoon olive oil
½ cup balsamic vinegar
2 tablespoons honey

Preheat the oven to 400°F and line a small baking sheet with parchment paper, aluminum foil, or a Silpat mat.

In a medium bowl, toss the carrots with the olive oil until they're well coated. Spread the carrots out on the prepared baking sheet so they don't touch. Roast them for about 30 minutes, or until the carrots are browned on the edges and tender.

While the carrots are roasting, heat a small saucepan or sauté pan over medium heat for 1 minute. Add the balsamic vinegar and honey. Stir well and bring to a simmer. Reduce the heat to low and simmer for about 8 to 10 minutes, or until the vinegar and honey are reduced to a thick, syrupy glaze. Be careful not to cook the glaze too long or it will burn.

When the carrots are done, drizzle them with the balsamic glaze and serve.

Last Bite Recipe:
Magnificent Minestrone Soup

Yield: 1–2 servings (freezes well and will keep frozen for up to 1 month)

Vegetables simmered with beans and pasta, minestrone is a great contribution from the Italians to comfort-food lovers everywhere. Serve it with crusty toasted bread and a salad.

1 tablespoon olive oil

2 tablespoons finely diced onions

1 tablespoon finely diced celery

1 tablespoon finely diced carrot

Flavor Blast!

2 teaspoons minced garlic

1 tablespoon minced fresh Italian parsley

2 teaspoons dried basil

1 teaspoon dried oregano

½ teaspoon dried thyme

1 (15-ounce) can tomatoes in juice

1 cup mixed vegetables diced or cut into small pieces, such as zucchini, yellow squash, green beans, peas, corn, peppers, and mushrooms

1 potato, peeled and diced into ¼-inch pieces

2 cups vegetable or chicken stock (or water)

Salt and freshly ground black pepper

1 (15-ounce) can white beans, drained and rinsed

3 tablespoons orzo (rice shaped pasta)

Heat a large saucepan over medium-high heat for 1 minute, add the olive oil, and wait for 30 seconds. When the oil is hot, add the onions, celery, and carrots and sauté for 3 to 4 minutes, or until the onions are starting to brown slightly. Add the *Flavor Blast!* ingredients (the garlic, Italian parsley, basil, oregano, and thyme) and sauté for 1 minute, allowing the herbs' volatile oils to be released.

Add the tomatoes, vegetables, potato, and stock. Reduce the heat to medium-low and let the soup simmer for about 30 minutes. Taste for seasoning and add salt and pepper if necessary. Reduce the heat to low, add the beans and orzo, and cook for another 10 minutes, or until the orzo is tender.

Ladle up and enjoy!

Recipe Notes

_____

_____

_____

_____

_____

_____

_____

_____

_____

_____

_____

_____

_____

_____

_____

Chapter 8

Is There Such a Thing as _Extra_ Desserts?!

In this chapter, we don't specifically list dessert recipes.

We're sure you have either a tried-and-true family favorite, some other recipe that you enjoy, or one that you have been meaning to try!

We just want to give some pointers and suggestions on what to do with leftover desserts you may have, so that there is no wasting. It's just a sin and a shame to not eat up every bite of desserts! ☺

Cookies

When mixing up a batch of cookies, you have a couple of easy options for not wasting. Using a small ice cream scoop, measure out individual portions onto a cookie sheet, put in the freezer to freeze up, and then put them in a bag. These can be frozen for up to 3 weeks and that way you easily have individual cookie portions you can take out of the freezer and pop in the oven! You can also freeze baked cookies. Put a scoop of your favorite ice cream between 2 of the thawed cookies and you've got a quick and easy ice cream sandwich!

Cookies are a great and easy way to have a little sweet treat after dinner, and they are super easy to have as an "every bite" dessert!

Fruit Pies

What do you do with a leftover fruit pie like apple or strawberry rhubarb? Now that's a tough one! An easy thing to do is take the remainder of the pie (crust and all), and freeze it. Then follow this easy recipe below to make a simple and tasty crumble:

Preheat oven to 250°F. Place the thawed fruit filling in an oven safe dish (the size of the dish will vary depending on the amount of filling you have). In a separate small bowl, combine the following until well mixed and crumbly: ¼ cup brown sugar, ¼ cup all-purpose flour, 2 tablespoons softened butter and ½ cup chopped pecans and walnuts (optional). Spoon the crumbly mixture over the filling. Place in oven and warm until the top is brown, about 20–25 minutes.

Tada! Pie 2.0

Cream Pies

For leftover cream pies like coconut cream or chocolate cream, save the filling portion only of the leftover pie and freeze for up to two weeks. Then when you need dessert, layer the thawed filling in a tall glass or martini glass with cake pieces in a trifle. A trifle is a layered dessert dish using a custard or cream filling, fruit and cake. It is a lovely way to display a dessert. No one would guess it's made from leftovers!

Brownies

Brownies are another great dessert that also gives you a lot of options for utilizing the leftovers. You can individually wrap leftover brownies in plastic wrap and then put them in are-sealable bag to freeze, or you can use leftover brownies later in a trifle. If using in a trifle, layer with chocolate pudding and whipped cream topping. Add some canned cherries as part of the layering for more of a "black forest" themed trifle.

Recipe Notes

Chapter 9

Lunches That Rock: Be the Envy of Your Co-workers

In this chapter, we focus on some ideas for taking delicious, nutritious, and cost-effective lunches to work with you. Some of the recipes build upon other recipes in the book (for example, Victory Garden Polenta Salad uses the Victory Garden Polenta with Tomato Sauce and Greens recipe from chapter 7 and makes it more of a lunch-friendly meal), and some are new, but still use some unused items from previous recipes.

Homemade lunches like these take a little bit of time to plan and prep, but they're so worth it!

Baby Kale Salad with Crispy Rice Cakes

Yield: 1 salad and 3 rice cakes (see notes at end of recipe regarding extra yield)

A tasty and easy twist on plain old rice; jazzed up *Every Bite*-style!

1 cup sushi rice (nishiki, calrose, or botan)*

1 egg

1 teaspoon cornstarch

½ tablespoon rice wine vinegar**

Flavor Blast!

2 tablespoons minced green onion, both white and green parts

Salt and freshly ground black pepper to taste

1 teaspoon fresh Italian parsley and/or chives—or any other herb leftover from a previous recipe

½ tablespoon sesame oil

Pinch of cayenne pepper (optional) or other fresh, hot pepper like jalapeno or Serrano; sliced thin (leave the seeds in for more heat)

1 tablespoon vegetable oil, for frying

½ recipe Baby Kale Salad with White Beans and Mustard Vinaigrette (page 145), salad left undressed***

Preparation at home

Cook the rice according to the package directions and allow it to cool for 20 minutes. Once complete, mix in the egg, cornstarch, rice wine vinegar and *Flavor Blast!* ingredients (the green onion, salt, pepper, sesame oil, herbs, and cayenne pepper, if using) and form the mixture into 2½-inch cakes.****

Heat the vegetable oil in a medium nonstick skillet for about 30 seconds on medium high heat. Fry cakes for about 1–3 minutes per side or until browned and crispy. Transfer it to a paper towel–lined plate to wick and excess oil, and let cool to room temperature.

Put the salad and dressing in separate "to go" containers.

At work

Warm the rice cake in the microwave until hot.

Toss the kale salad with beans and the vinaigrette dressing. Serve with the crispy cakes on top.

Be prepared to answer questions from coworkers about your AMAZING lunch.

Notes From Within Recipe

*We use sushi rice in this recipe because it sticks together to form a nice-shaped patty. No sushi rice on hand? No problem! You can certainly use any rice you have.

**Rice wine vinegar is a little sweeter than other vinegars, but you can use what you have on hand. Don't have any vinegar? Use lemon or lime juice.

***Store the dressing in a separate container until lunch, so the salad doesn't wilt.

****The cakes can be made up to this point and frozen for up to 3 weeks. Just thaw and fry them.

Victory Garden Polenta Salad

Yield: 1 salad

Use some of the polenta from Victory Garden Polenta with Tomato Sauce and Greens (recipe page 137) to make a tasty salad that is hearty enough to hold you through the day.

½ recipe polenta from Victory Garden Polenta with Tomato Sauce and Greens (see recipe, page 137), cooled completely(or other polenta)

1 tablespoon vegetable or canola oil

1 cup salad greens (any variety/combination) and any leftover veggies from previous recipes you want to include

2 tablespoons Mustard Vinaigrette (see recipe, page 147), Balsamic Vinaigrette (page 183), or other dressing

Preparation at home

Cut the polenta into bite-sized pieces. Heat the oil in a medium nonstick pan over medium-high heat for about a minute. Add the polenta pieces and fry until crispy on all sides. Transfer it to a paper towel–lined plate to drain, and let cool to room temperature.

Put the salad greens, vegetables (if any), and dressing in separate "to go" containers.

At work

Briefly heat the polenta pieces in the microwave for about one minute or until just warm.

Toss the salad with the vegetables (if any), and the dressing. Top the salad with the polenta pieces.

Black Bean Soup with Braised Greens and Rice

Yield: 4 servings (can be refrigerated and/or frozen into individual portions)

Black Bean Soup is a great, hearty soup. Easy to make over the weekend and take it for lunch during the week. Leftovers also freeze nicely!

Make it complete by serving with Two Alarm Braised Greens and Rice (see recipe, page 148) mixed together with Heavenly Herbed Rice (see recipe, page 155). They make a nice accompaniment to the soup and bread.

2 teaspoon olive oil

1 small onion, about ¾ cup—diced into ¼-inch pieces

1 green or red bell pepper, about 1 cup—stemmed, seeded, and diced into ¼-inch pieces

1 rib celery, about ½ cup—diced into ¼-inch pieces

2 cloves minced garlic

1 (15-ounce) can tomatoes in juice

1st Flavor Blast!
2 teaspoons ground cumin
2 teaspoons sweet paprika
1 teaspoon oregano—Mexican if possible
Dash of salt and freshly ground pepper

3½ cups chicken or vegetable stock (or water)

2 (15-ounce) cans black beans, rinsed and drained

2nd Flavor Blast! (per serving)
1/8 teaspoon ground cumin
1 tablespoon sour cream (or low fat or non fat yogurt)
1/8 teaspoon chopped fresh cilantro (extra from a previous recipe); optional

2 slices good crusty bread

Side dish of Two Alarm Braised Greens and Rice (see recipe page 148)—optional

Preparation at home

In a sturdy 3 quart pot, heat the olive oil over medium heat for 1 minute. Add the onion, bell pepper, celery, and garlic, and sauté until tender, about 4 to 5 minutes. Reduce the heat to medium-low. Add the *Flavor Blast!* ingredients (the cumin, paprika, oregano, salt, and pepper), and sauté for 1 minute to open up the volatile oils in the seasonings and to release their flavor. Add the diced tomatoes and sauté 2 minutes more. Add the stock (or water) and beans; mixing well, and simmer for 25 minutes. Stir occasionally and taste for seasonings, adding more salt and pepper if needed.

While the soup is simmering, prepare an individual serving of the *2nd Flavor Blast* (the cumin, sour cream, and cilantro—if using). Stir together and put in a small "to go" container.

Pour the soup into a blender and puree (or use a hand blender). Once the soup is blended to your desired consistency, return it to the pot and warm it over low heat.* Let simmer for 15 minutes. Turn off and let cool.

Lightly toast your bread, let cool, and place in a "to go" bag.

Pour ¼ of the soup into a thermos or other "to go" container.

At work

Heat the soup in a bowl in the microwave for 1 minute and stir. If not warm enough, heat for another 30–45 seconds (time might vary a little depending on if the soup was kept warmer longer in a thermos, as opposed to a "to go" container). Top with a dollop of the *2ⁿᵈ Flavor Blast!*

Enjoy with your good crusty bread and braised greens and rice if you brought them along!

Note From Within Recipe

*A creative and different way to incorporate any leftover Braised Greens and Rice you might have is to add them directly to the pureed black bean soup. Adding the rice in gives it a little extra heartiness and is similar to our Beef Barley soup recipe and our Revitalizing Rice and Vegetable Stew recipe in that way.

Pear and Blue Cheese Salad with Balsamic Vinaigrette

Yield: 1 serving

Pear and blue cheese is a match made in heaven! The combo has such wonderful contrast: the crispness of the pear and the creaminess of the blue cheese. Divine!

2 cup mixed baby greens
2 tablespoons Balsamic Vinaigrette Dressing (recipe follows)
1 pear, halved, cored, and thinly sliced lengthwise (preparation done at work)
1 tablespoon crumbled blue cheese
1 tablespoon walnuts, toasted and chopped*

Preparation at home:

Prepare your "to go" container with the greens, blue cheese, and walnuts. Prepare separate containers for the pear and prepared dressing.

At work:

Slice the pear and add to the prepared salad. Add the dressing and lightly toss. You're ready to enjoy a delicious salad!

Notes From Within Recipe

*To toast nuts, heat a small pan over medium-low heat. Gently stir while the nuts begin to brown in color and they begin to create an aroma, about 5–7 minutes. Be sure not to leave them unattended, as nuts can brown (and potentially burn) very quickly!

Balsamic Vinaigrette Dressing

Yield: ¼ cup

This vinaigrette will keep, tightly covered, in the refrigerator for up to a week and is a lovely accompaniment to any salad! Recipe will easily double or triple.

1 tablespoon balsamic vinegar
1 teaspoon Dijon mustard
¼ finely minced garlic clove
¼ cup olive oil
Salt and freshly ground black pepper

In a small bowl, whisk to combine the vinegar, mustard, and garlic. Add the oil in a slow steady stream, whisking constantly. Season with salt and pepper to taste. Or use a hand blender by combining everything but the oil. Then add the oil as you run the hand blender. This will take about 1 minute to make.

Castaway Salad

Yield: 1 serving

Cast those leftover veggies from the fridge into this salad for a healthy and delicious lunch.

1 cup greens (anything you have in the fridge)

½ cup total of any or all of the following you might have in your fridge, cut into small pieces: small ripe tomato, cucumber, cauliflower, carrot, bell pepper, mushrooms, or fennel (fronds and/or bulb)

1 tablespoon softened and crumbled goat cheese (or any other cheese left from a previous recipe)

2 tablespoons Mustard Vinaigrette (see recipe, page 147), Balsamic Vinaigrette (see recipe, page 183), or other dressing

Preparation at home:

Toss the greens together with the various vegetables in your "to go" container. Prepare a separate, smaller container for your prepared dressing.

At work:

Toss the prepared salad with the dressing and enjoy!

Recipe Notes

Chapter 10

Snacks
Eating Healthy in Between Meals

In this chapter, we offer a few ideas to help you get through the day in a healthy and tasty way. You'll definitely enjoy Every Bite of these delicious snacks!

Power Boost Bars

Yield: 10 (2-ounce) bars

These bars will give you that extra boost of power when you need it. Make them over the weekend, and you have a great snack to enjoy throughout the week, or you can freeze some and make them last up to a month.

1 cup quick-cooking oats
1 cup chopped dates
1 cup raw pumpkin seeds
½ cup raw sunflower seeds
½ cup peanut butter (chunky or smooth)
¼ cup plus 2 tablespoons raw honey (plus slightly more or less if needed)

In a large bowl, mix all the ingredients except the honey until well combined and evenly distributed. Stir in the honey and squeeze a handful of the mixture; it should hold together in your hand. If it doesn't, add a little more honey, about a ½ teaspoon at a time, until everything holds together.

Press the mixture into a large baking dish lined with plastic wrap or parchment paper. Pat it to a uniform thickness of about ½ inch.

Cut into 10 bars and wrap them individually in plastic wrap, and then in a well-sealed bag. Well sealed, they will keep for about 2 weeks at room temperature.

Easy Trail Mix

Yield: 4 cups

You don't have to be hiking to enjoy this tasty trail mix! Most, if not all, of these ingredients can be found in the bulk foods section of your grocery store. Utilize the bulk foods section to only get what you need to minimize waste.

1 cup roasted, salted soy nuts
1 cup dried pineapple slices*
½ cup unsweetened shredded coconut
½ cup chopped candied ginger
½ cup banana chips, broken up into bite-size pieces
½ cup dark chocolate chips

In a large bowl, mix all the ingredients until well combined and evenly distributed. Divide into ½-cup portions, place in individual bags, and you're ready to go!**

Notes From Within Recipe

* Some specialty stores and/or grocery stores have freeze-dried, unsweetened pineapple pieces. Feel free to use those instead!

** Trail mix will keep at least 2 weeks in well-sealed bags.

Seize the Day Drink

Yield: 1 smoothie

Too busy to cook breakfast? Seize the day with this super-easy smoothie that will get your day started right! You can also make it in the afternoon to give yourself a little lift.

½ frozen banana, peeled*
½ cup frozen strawberries*
1 tablespoon goji berries**
1 slice peeled fresh ginger (about the size and thickness of a quarter)***
2 tablespoons protein powder supplement
½ cup yogurt (low fat, nonfat, or flavored)****
4 medium fresh mint leaves (optional)*****

In a blender, combine everything and blend until smooth, about 1 to 2 minutes. Enjoy immediately.

Notes From Within Recipe

* When you have bananas or strawberries getting overripe and about to go bad, don't throw them away! Throw them in the freezer for use in this smoothie (you can certainly use fresh strawberries and banana). For extra frozen bananas you might have, you can use them in banana bread, or puree them in a blender with a little cream or milk for an easy and quick "ice cream".

** Goji berries are packed with vitamins and antioxidants, and are considered a "superfood". Dried berries are most commonly found at health food markets, the bulk foods section of your local grocery store, or you can order them online.

If you can't easily find them, it's okay to leave them out. You'll still have a great smoothie!

***Ginger can also be frozen. Simply throw it in a bag to use in your next recipe.

****Freeze any leftover yogurt as well and use it later (with a leftover banana perhaps) to make an easy smoothie.

*****Mint leaves give this drink a refreshing brightness. Store fresh mint by sniping the stem ends and keeping them in about 1 inch of water in a glass in the refrigerator, and cover loosely with a plastic bag. Fresh mint will keep about one week like this. You can also puree the mint and freeze it in super small containers or ice cube trays. Just drop a frozen cube in the smoothies before pureeing.

Recipe Notes

Chapter 11

Supplemental Recipes

In this chapter, we add on a few extra recipes that are referenced earlier in the cookbook.

Zippy Tomato Sauce

Yield: about 1½ cups

A delicious and quick, all-purpose tomato sauce. This is an easy way to make a fantastic sauce and is one of those great "base recipes" to have in your culinary tool box!

1 tablespoon olive oil
2 teaspoons minced fresh Italian parsley
2 cloves garlic, smashed flat as a piece of paper
1 (15-ounce) can of <u>best quality</u> whole tomatoes in juice
½ teaspoon salt
¼ teaspoon freshly ground black pepper

Heat a medium saucepan on medium high heat for 1 minute. Add the olive oil and heat 30 seconds. Add the smashed garlic cloves and the parsley and sauté until the garlic just starts to brown, about 2 minutes. Add the tomatoes and juice and reduce the heat to medium. Season with the salt and freshly ground black pepper and stir and smash the tomatoes while they cook. Continue to smash and stir until a nice chunky sauce is made, about 8 minutes. Taste for seasoning and adjust as needed.

Basic Vinaigrette Dressing

Yield: ¾ cup

Another great "basic recipe" to have that you can use on just about anything!

2 ounces vinegar*
6 ounces olive oil
2 teaspoons Dijon mustard
1 teaspoon dry basil**
½ teaspoon salt
¼ teaspoon freshly ground pepper

In a small bowl, mix the vinegar, Dijon mustard, and basil together. While whisking vigorously, add the olive in a very thin stream. As the vinaigrette thickens you can add the oil slightly faster. Season with salt and pepper.

Store in the refrigerator for up to a week.

Notes From Within Recipe

*You can use any vinegar such as the classic white distilled variety, or kick it up a notch and try one with a little more flavor to it such as champagne vinegar.

**if you have some fresh basil left over from another recipe, simply mince it up (1 tablespoon's worth) and add it in. Either one will be lovely! Dill would also work nicely in this dressing if you have that on hand.

Fabulous Flaky Pie Crust

Yield: dough for two 9-inch pie crusts

3 cups all-purpose flour
1½ teaspoons salt
1 cup shortening
1 egg, beaten
1 teaspoon vinegar*
½ cup ice water

Combine flour and salt in a large bowl. Cut, shortening into flour mixture with a pastry blender** until the mixture resembles coarse meal. In a separate smaller bowl, combine the egg, vinegar, and ice water. Gradually add this wet mixture to the dry ingredients; mixing until the dough holds its shape. Form into a large ball, and split evenly in two. Flatten each half into a disk shape, wrap in plastic wrap and place in the refrigerator to let it rest for at least 30 minutes before using.***

Variation: to make an Herbed Flaky Crust for a savory dish, add 2 tablespoons total of minced fresh herbs (any combination you have on hand) or 1½ teaspoons of dried herbs. Add the herbs in when first mixing the flour and salt together, and proceed with the rest of the recipe as written.

Notes From Within Recipe

*White, distilled vinegar is preferred, as it doesn't have as much of a taste as others such as apple cider vinegar.

**If you don't have a pastry blender on hand, you can use two butter knives to cut the shortening into the flour. Hold a knife in each hand and cut through the shortening until it resembles coarse meal.

***When mixing flour and water together to make a pastry, it begins to form gluten strands. The more gluten strands form, the heavier the pastry. To prevent that (and to keep the pastry as light and flaky as possible), we try to reduce forming those gluten strands. One way is to not knead the dough with your hands. The heat from your hands will heat up the dough slightly and will cause more gluten to form. That is why the recipe calls for using a pastry blender or butter knives to mix the dough. Another way to help keep the pastry cool is by using ice water. Be sure your water is very cold before you start making up this dough. Finally, resting the dough before using it allows any of the gluten stands that have formed to relax out in the pastry.

All these things will help you have the best, most fabulously flaky pie crust ever!

Recipe Notes

_____

_____

_____

_____

_____

_____

_____

_____

_____

_____

_____

_____

_____

_____

_____

_____